ASK A NATIVE NEW YORKER

HARD-EARNED ADVICE ON SURVIVING AND THRIVING IN THE BIG CITY

JAKE DOBKIN

Abrams Image, New York

Editor: David Cashion
Designer: Danielle Youngsmith
Production Manager: Denise LaCongo

Library of Congress Control Number: 2018936288

ISBN: 978-1-4197-2908-9
eISBN: 978-1-68335-497-0

Printed and bound in USA
10 9 8 7 6 5 4 3 2 1

Abrams Image books are available at special discounts when purchased in
quantity for premiums and promotions as well as fundraising or educational
use. Special editions can also be created to specification. For details, contact
specialsales@abramsbooks.com or the address below.

Abrams Image® is a registered trademark of Harry N. Abrams, Inc.

ABRAMS The Art of Books
195 Broadway, New York, NY 10007
abramsbooks.com

This book is dedicated to everyone who has ever moved to
New York and tried to make a life here—it really is an act of spiritual
bravery, no matter how it turns out—and especially to Karen,
who moved here in 1994, took a chance on dating a native New Yorker,
and eventually became the mother to two more.

Contents

The true New Yorker
secretly believes that
people living anywhere
else have to be, in
some sense, kidding.

—JOHN UPDIKE

Introduction

Every year, thousands of people move to New York City completely ignorant of how this place works. They pour into the greatest and most complex city this planet has ever produced, and most soon realize they've got no clear idea how to survive here, let alone thrive. After a few months or a few years, worn down by urban stress and high rent, they declare defeat and leave.

I've lived here my whole life, and after observing this process year after year, I got to thinking: What a waste of time and effort! What's more, it's an entirely avoidable one. With a little guidance, these kids could have blossomed into lifelong residents of the best city in the world, and instead, because no one ever got real with them about how to make it here, they're on a bus back to Akron, or worse, on a plane to Los Angeles, which has a long history of luring people whom New York has destroyed.

I think of it this way: If you had to move to the Amazon Rainforest, would you just wade right into the river looking for a fish to eat? Of course not, because you'd immediately get your feet chewed off by piranhas. No, before you did anything, you'd try to get the lay of the land. You could try to scrape together some insight from Google and Wikipedia, but that's obviously a poor substitute for locating a native guide to show you around—someone who has survived in that environment since birth and been made wise by the experience.

But locating a native New Yorker willing to spend any time with a newcomer is difficult: Decades of gentrification have decimated the population of natives throughout the city, and, because of that, the locals who do remain tend to be somewhat closed off to strangers, holed up in out-of-the-way neighborhoods, mainly socializing with friends and family who are lifers like themselves. So I've decided to offer myself—one real deal, loudmouthed denizen of the Big Apple—to help you, the new arrival, get your shit straight.

Why me? I'm a third-generation native New Yorker, raised by a typical New York family of radical leftist Jews and seasoned on the not-so-mean streets of Park Slope, Brooklyn, back when it was first revitalizing in the 1980s. After eighteen years in the public school system, I went to college at Columbia. And, after my brief career in the dot-com boom was cut short by the dot-com crash, I found myself at NYU for business school, where I used my student loans to cofound Gothamist, a website about New York City. For more than fifteen years I managed that publication as it expanded to four million monthly readers as we explored every crease and crevice of New York City.

Most of our staffers are young, relatively recent arrivals to the city, and over time, I found I enjoyed answering their questions about life here. Come to think of it, sometimes they didn't even ask the questions; I just volunteered my advice unsolicited, in the true native style. Observing this, Gothamist's editor in chief, John Del Signore, finally suggested I take questions from our readers as well, and over the last few years I've answered more than 150 of them in columns on the site.

This book isn't a repackaging of that material, however—I wanted to start over from scratch and answer a new set of questions designed specifically for the edification of new arrivals, their friends, and other natives who like to give advice. Each one is based in whole or in part on a question I've actually received, but most have been boiled down to what I believe is the central quandary of the author. It is inevitable that in some places I have repeated phrases or ideas that I explored online, but I have attempted to make this book as close to new as possible.

Who is a *native New Yorker*? This deceptively simple question is the first one we need to answer before we can move on to anything more substantial. After all, you need to be sure you've got the right guy advising you here.

First, it's the geography. It is indisputably true that New York City is composed of the five boroughs of Manhattan, Brooklyn, Queens, the Bronx, and Staten Island. No one born outside these lands, say in Westchester, on Long Island, or in Northern New Jersey, may claim to be a native New Yorker. People will often do this with a quick "I'm from New York," but this is a lie of omission. What they mean is that they are from the New York suburbs, and they know about as much about New York City as the average tourist. If you're not sure you're dealing with a true native, ask, "What neighborhood did you grow up in?" The fakes always offer a nervous pause and then say something like "Scarsdale—it's like twenty minutes outside the city."

Within the city, this book posits that all natives are equal. Some will claim that their particular neighborhood has a deeper claim to native bragging rights than the others, but this is just self-flattery. Yes, experiences of New York differ widely—some areas are very rich, others are very poor, some are diverse, and some are very segregated, but none can claim a deeper understanding of the city—just a unique one. A native who grew up in Tottenville in Staten Island, which is very far from Manhattan, surely has not had the same experiences as one who grew up in Bed-Stuy, Brooklyn, but—and this is important—their perspectives offer equally valid types of native wisdom, which we must honor and try to learn from.

In this book, I will of course give answers influenced by my own particular upbringing in the city and try, where I think my views are sufficiently different from those of my fellow natives, to give some other perspectives. But on most issues of importance, like when to pull the emergency brake on the subway or how to handle noisy neighbors, I believe most natives will tend to agree, and I will simply speak for the group.

So, is a native someone who was simply born within the city limits? No—this is necessary but not sufficient. There are two more requirements, of increasing difficulty. The first is that the putative native must not have left the city for any significant length of time. Vacations are fine—apart from a few rumored inhabitants of Staten Island who have supposedly never set foot on the mainland, most natives will have, of course, left occasionally to travel, if only to be reminded of how much worse every other place is compared to home.

For how long are you allowed to leave and still be considered a native? Duration doesn't matter as much as intention: If the native always intends to return home, he or she may leave for months—even years. The longer the person spends away, however, the more doubtful we must be of their intention to go back. A summer trip, fine. A trip around the world, probably okay. Four years at college? Maybe, although that's starting to stretch it. Ten years overseas for work? Probably not; the true native would have found a different job in the city rather than relocate for that long. Personally, the longest I ever got away was for ten weeks during a college study abroad in Spain. My takeaway: Many European cities are very beautiful, but not one has half the vitality of New York on its most boring day.

But let's say you were born here and never left except for occasional trips. Are you a native New Yorker? Not quite: There's one final thing you must do, and that's die here. Every native is provisional until they finally go the way of all flesh, having never moved away. After all, if you retire to Florida, we can agree that your love for New York City was not strong enough to overcome your hatred for New York winters, for example—and you are certainly not as truly native as someone who survives polar vortices as an octogenarian. It also helps, for bonus points, if you can arrange to have your remains interred here, maybe by having your body laid to rest in one of those graveyards by the Long Island Expressway in Queens, or, as is my plan, by having your ashes scattered in the Gowanus Canal.

This is a harsh truth, and you may be thinking, "Come on, Jake, even you do not meet this final qualification." Not yet, I agree. True nativity is a platonic ideal that can only be aimed for, but not achieved, during life. But I aspire to expire here, and I say that goes for every true native in the city. So let's just agree that I'm about as native as you can get while still incarnate, and if, at some later date, I am forced by climate change or war or other apocalypse to leave the city, I will issue a sincere apology and include it in a later edition of this book.

A related question that people who move to New York often ask me is, "How long must I stay until I am considered native?" The answer is this: Unless you were born here, you will never be a native, and that's a nonnegotiable fact. However, that doesn't mean you can't be a "real" New

Yorker. Like nativity, "realness" has its own definition. In fact, it has many definitions. Some people say you're a real New Yorker the second you get off Amtrak with your bags, intending, like so many before you, to find your place here. Others say it happens when you have a certain New York experience: getting mugged on the street, maybe, or paying too much to rent your first apartment. Some argue that realness grows with time, and after a year or ten years, you can declare victory. I say all of these things are true—"real" is a subjective title you must eventually award yourself after you've achieved sufficient personal victories and defeats here and built up enough New York wisdom that you no longer need a book like this one. In fact, you could say that's the purpose of this book: to help you manifest your true New York realness.

How will you know when you have achieved this milestone? Here's a clue: Real New Yorkers do not ask others if they are real New Yorkers— they just know. What's more, they can't help themselves from judging other people's realness and finding it lacking. When you get to this point— you jaywalk instinctively, can give complicated directions to tourists in the West Village, watch a rat crawl over a sleeping subway rider's face without screaming, and find yourself giving advice to new arrivals with that seen-it-all voice that all real New Yorkers have—that's when you know you truly belong here and probably won't ever be moving anywhere else.

That's important: Like natives, real New Yorkers do not leave. That does not mean they never contemplate leaving—even natives occasionally do that, if only to laugh at the idea. New York will always be a tough place to live (but as we will explore in the next chapter, that's one of the great things about it) and that toughness can lead anyone with alternatives to consider getting out. But the real New Yorkers never do. Somehow, they always find a way to keep going here, right to the end of their lives. If you're doing that, or trying to do that, you're a real enough New Yorker for me.

CHAPTER 1

Why Is New York the Greatest City in the World?

Once you have lived
in New York and it has
become your home,
no place else is good
enough.

—JOHN STEINBECK

Dear Jake,

I'm facing a serious life decision, and I'm not sure what to do. The basic facts: I am graduating from college this year (from a Midwestern university with a stereotypical liberal arts degree). I've got two options for what to do after school: I could move back to Minneapolis, or I could move to New York. I've got internship offers in both cities—both at media companies. Back home I've got family and friends, but I'm worried I'll feel bored. In New York, I only know two acquaintances from school, and the longest I've ever visited was for a week during a family trip. I loved visiting but I'm intimidated and freaking out a little about actually moving there. What would you advise: Stick to what I know or take the leap and move out east?

Sincerely,
Not in Kansas Anymore

Dear NIKA,

You should move to New York! Everyone who has the opportunity should move to New York. The only route to self-realization is through challenge, and there is no place more challenging and exhilarating to live. Five months in this urban crucible will give you insight into the human experience that would take five years to gain in Minneapolis. Spend five years here, and you will discover things about yourself and about humankind that many people outside New York don't learn in a lifetime.

You are right to be nervous: Moving to New York is one of the hardest moves there is. Of all the cities in America, it is one of the most expensive to live in, and simply finding a reasonable apartment to inhabit can be a costly ordeal. Then there are the physical tests: A human brain accustomed to the civilized quiet of the Midwest will take several weeks to adjust to the incessant noise, pungent odors, and stampeding crowds here. And all that is before you actually settle down to the work of finding a real job, true friends, and a purpose for your life.

To take such a risk requires suitable rewards. Other new arrivals have probably told you of the myriad riches to be found here. Many are drawn to the sheer beauty of this city: the skyline at sunset, or the way the first or last light of the day perfectly aligns with the grid on Manhattanhenge, or the mornings when fog hangs low over the river and the skyscrapers seem to levitate above the ground. For others, it's the cultural treasures: world-class museums, galleries, theaters, and music venues that can fill endless weekends. And, of course, the overabundance of culinary offerings, from four-star restaurants to sidewalk food stands in Queens with chefs from every country on Earth.

What about the convenience of having twenty-four-hour everything, from subways to supermarkets? (And being able to get pretty much anything your heart desires delivered right to your doorstep?) Or what a relief it is to be able to walk almost everywhere, which makes so many things in life easier, including going out for drinks with your friends and not having to drive home drunk at four in the morning?

Plus, there is the feeling of awe knowing that the streets you're walking down are the very places where so much of American culture was born: hip-hop, graffiti, photography, virtually all the best American novels, poems, and plays.

But maybe you are more focused on the practical stuff, like landing a desirable job. No other city has as many career options or vibrant industries—not just finance and media, which are what New York tends to be known for—but trades like fashion, tech, tourism, healthcare, and dozens of others that are being invented right now in our warehouses and laboratories. Sure, it's expensive here, and you'll be living in a closet, but if you persevere, you'll likely make more money doing more interesting work than you could just about anywhere else.

These are all popular reasons to consider moving to NYC, especially if you're from somewhere where you can't get a real slice of pizza at 3 A.M., but, from the perspective of a native, they are not the real reasons for moving here. The aforementioned rationales are all about entertaining or rewarding the self, and the stuff you gain from them—money, status, cultural expertise—is not integral to the character that defines the real New York experience.

I want to return to the challenges of living here: the noise, the odors, and crowds. Add to those a few more: the constant clash, physical and spiritual, of our city's different cultures and classes; the lines for everything; the high costs and taxes, not just of housing but of everything. The threat of terrorism, real or imagined, the pervasive filth—debauched rats having orgies on garbage piles and trash-strewn subway tracks bursting into flames. The hellish heat in summer and the bitter cold in winter. The presence of weirdos of all types—street performers, tourists, financiers, emotionally disturbed people screaming on street corners. Also, traffic blocking half the streets in the city and agitated drivers leaning on their horns. Oh, and bedbugs, we have those too—swarms of bloodthirsty bedbugs.

You might be thinking, *Jake, those sound like reasons* not *to move to NYC*, but I am going to argue that the chance to face these challenges and provocations, and overcome them, more than all those superficial appealing advantages people usually talk about, is what makes New York the place you want to call home. There are many cities where you can find a good job and some culture, but few where you can do it while learning to maintain your equanimity in a maelstrom like this.

So what does living in New York teach you?

First, it teaches you courage. From the moment you get off the bus, train, or plane, the city stages an assault on the senses. At the beginning, this will feel unremitting—the regular earthquakes triggered by passing trucks, the bone-rattling banging of the jackhammers, the fetid stench of the streets in summer, the curse of the dreaded poop train. Simply getting used to this stuff requires you to develop nerves of steel. The same goes for navigating the subway system late at night; or going to work in one of our skyscrapers, knowing what happened on 9/11; or immersing yourself in a sea of strangers in a new neighborhood.

Over time, you'll find spiritual courage follows physical resilience. It takes a lot of grit to apply for jobs despite knowing you're facing competition from the whole city, or to try and score a good apartment despite knowing how hard it is to find one and how much you're going to overpay. It takes some moxie to find friends and romantic partners in a city with millions of alternatives—and spiritual strength to stick with them in good times and bad.

Second, you will learn a newfound appreciation for justice and fairness. After moving here, you'll find the only way this many people can get along without immediate bloodshed is a scrupulous sense for treating others (reasonably) well. Act like a jerk in New York—push your way to the front of a line, take up more than your fair share of space on the subway, snap too many pictures of your food while you're out at one of our restaurants—and see what happens. The harsh backlash you will experience is a manifestation of the uniquely strong regard in which New Yorkers hold the golden rule.

You'll soon feel it too—maybe a little bit the first time someone tries to exit a bus at the front instead of the back, and more strongly the first time you step in dog poop that some inconsiderate human "forgot" to scoop up. Reading our local papers and websites will fan the flames: The stories they love the most are ones in which the rich and powerful get taken down a peg, like when a C-list celebrity gets caught demanding special treatment at the airport security lines by hissing, "Don't you know who I am?" You'll know you've really got the hang of it when you find yourself screaming at a stranger "What, you think you're special or something?" for some minor lapse of courtesy.

Third, a strong sense of self—of knowing who you are and what you want. You see, in this city you can have anything. You want an ice cream cone at 2 A.M. on Thanksgiving Day? No problem. You want to drink yourself sick at 7 A.M. on a Tuesday? We have countless options for you. Want to feel hopeless with envy? There are an endless number of people here who will be richer, more famous, or more powerful than you to compare yourself to. You can indulge every type of sin in New York. Whatever your preferred poison is, we have it in bottomless supply.

But you're not going to do that. Why? Because it's all so available, you're going to quickly learn what is good for you and what is not, or you're rapidly going to end up in rehab or worse. Moderation in the face of endless temptation will be one of the first signs of your growing maturity—when your friends ask you to go out on a Tuesday and you say, "Nah, I'm just going to stay in and read Joseph Mitchell." At first it might feel like a missed opportunity, but soon you'll achieve that I-don't-give-a-fuck attitude that real New Yorkers have, and you won't mind it at all.

Fourth, and finally, you will develop the wisdom that only surviving in New York for a long period of time can give you. This will manifest as a distinctly unique New York sense of humor: the ability to joke about any hardship or challenge—impending hurricanes, getting evicted, watching a rat eat a pigeon on a park bench. Many world religions believe acceptance of impermanence is the key to spiritual maturity, and there is nowhere you can learn this lesson better than here. The real New Yorker has been buffeted by change on all sides—neighborhoods transforming, friends coming to the city and leaving again, breaking various limbs in accidents you can only have in NYC, e.g., slipping on a bialy or falling down subway stairs. It will take years, and many successes and failures, to attain this knowledge. No success is more dizzying than New York success, and no failure is more black and terrible than New York failure.

You will spin around often, and you will, at least once and probably many times, curse your choice to come here, but sooner or later you will emerge enlightened. At that point, looking back over the New York terrain you've covered, you'll find that you agree with me: No other place would have been as difficult, and no other place could have been as great. Your friends back home will be awed, or at least weirded out, by the urban knowledge you've gained. "She's a New Yorker now," they'll quietly remark one fine night from behind the impenetrable walls of their Cheesecake Factory menus.

(One objection you may have is, "If struggle is the key to wisdom when choosing a place to live, why not just move to Somalia?" The answer, of course, is that there are probably very few good bagel places in Mogadishu right now, plus, when picking a city, you want to find a place that has the maximum challenge without a high likelihood of getting you killed.)

As a native, I'm jealous of your opportunity to decide whether New York is the right place for you, and of your chance to come here and try to make it. While we lifers have many advantages—for instance, uninterrupted access to phenomenal pizza—we will never have the opportunity to make a free choice to live here. That decision was made by our parents, or grandparents, or great-grandparents decades ago. And once you're born here, grow up here, and everything you know is here, the choice to live here really isn't a choice at all.

So, my friend, as someone faced with an option to come or go, you have my admiration. And if that, plus the other stuff we've discussed here, isn't enough to convince you to move to New York, let me add one more idea. As far as I know, you only get one life, and most people on this planet are cursed to spend it seeing only a tiny portion of the possibilities this universe offers. New York is one of the few places where you can experience almost all of these possibilities at once—every culture, every human interaction, every emotion—in the shortest period of time.

It is probably safer to stay in the Midwest, but won't some part of you always wonder what would've happened if you did move here? Don't condemn yourself to a lifetime of doubt; give New York your best shot.

Sincerely,
Jake

N.B.: Be careful when discussing this question with friends and family members who do not have the opportunity or inclination to move to the Big Apple. New York can provoke strong feelings in people from other places—fear, anger, hatred. Some of this comes from their suspicion, usually correct, that New Yorkers believe every other place is inferior, and some of it comes from their secret belief that New Yorkers might be right. Unless they've lived here themselves, best to avoid the subject entirely.

Five Most Important Locals to Befriend

---

1   **YOUR BUILDING'S SUPER.** The next time your ceiling is leaking at 4 A.M., you'll understand why. Tip them during the holidays.

2   **BODEGA PROPRIETOR.** It will help the next time you're one dollar short on a six-pack, but also for a range of other services, like neighborhood gossip and backup key storage.

3   **CAB DRIVERS.** Your life is in their hands. Be respectful and friendly and feel free to strike up a conversation instead of staring at your phone. Cab drivers are the eyes and ears of NYC, and they often have stories to tell of places you've never been—you can learn a lot from them!

4   **THE PEOPLE WHO DELIVER YOUR MAIL AND PACKAGES.** A friendly mail carrier or UPS delivery person will ensure your packages reach you unharmed. Give them a smile and show your gratitude.

5   **ROOMMATE.** Maybe this cramped living arrangement is not ideal, and maybe you'd both rather be on your own. But you either make the best of it by finding common ground, or see your home life devolve into a "Did he pee on my toothbrush?" nightmare. Your call.

CHAPTER 2

How to Recognize a Real New Yorker

Questions

I wake up every morning and say to myself, "Well, I'm still in New York. Thank you, God."

—FORMER NYC MAYOR ED KOCH

Dear Jake,

I moved to the city two weeks ago, and there are still many things I do not understand! For instance, how do I swipe a MetroCard in the subway or on the bus so it works without having to do it five times? But my biggest problem so far has been walking down the street. Yes, you heard me right. At least three times I've been walking along, just minding my own business, when someone sighs furiously or gruffly yells, "Excuse me!" and then rushes ahead. This has generally been on crowded streets in Manhattan, but it's happened at least once going up an escalator in the subway. What am I doing wrong? And why do New Yorkers walk so fast?

Please advise,
Walking Wrong

Dear WW,

New Yorkers do not walk too fast: You walk too slow. Most likely you grew up in a place where people got around in cars, which means your walking muscles are weak compared with those of people who get everywhere on foot. We also know where we're going, which makes us appear to be moving faster, but really, it's just that you are lost half the time, stopping to get your bearings, or else looking up to admire the skyscrapers we stopped being impressed by many years ago.

Give it six months—by then your body will have been honed by walking the standard five miles a day that most New Yorkers do during their daily routine, including the many flights of stairs required by most subway commutes and walk-up apartment buildings. During this time, you will also learn to move with the purpose of the experienced New Yorker: never stopping in the middle of a block to look at your phone for directions or to marvel at some routine New York sight—a red-faced Alec Baldwin screaming into his cell phone about dry-cleaning receipts, a guy in an Elmo costume smoking a cigarette, two cabbies having a fistfight over a fender bender, etc.

Learning to walk like a New Yorker is a vital skill. During your stay here, you will be constantly pressed for time. The unacceptable state of our subways and buses—which have been starved of necessary infrastructure funding for years by New York's car-crazy governors—means getting to work is always a game of Russian roulette, so you'll often find yourself running from the station to your job. Then there's work itself, where the hours will be long partly because of the workaholism of our intensely competitive industries, but also because most New Yorkers need to put in maximum hours to make enough money to pay our exorbitant rents. This leaves twenty minutes for lunch, which requires getting to the deli fast because there will also be ten people on line when you get there. If you have to bark at a waddling tourist or two along the way, so be it.

Even at night, when you'd think people would slow down, they don't. Most New Yorkers are either rushing home to see their friends and family during the small amount of free time left to them after work, or they're trying to get to whatever restaurant/bar/club they just heard about, and they either need to get there early to beat the crowd, or—even when they do score a reservation—they know that if they're even five minutes late, they're going to lose it. So, no matter what, they're still going to walk fast.

For similar reasons, being punctual is a much more important virtue in New York City than in other places in America. We have far less free time and we don't want it wasted, so being constantly late is treated as a much more serious character flaw. Of course, we forgive an occasional delay caused by a comatose G train or some such unavoidable problem, but do it often and you will soon find yourself very unpopular here.

Some advice to help you get up to local speed:

First, and most importantly, figure out where you're going before you step into the stream of human traffic. It's like merging onto a busy highway in a Fiat: This is not the time to suddenly stop and look at a map, fumble for your phone to text your friend, or realize that you're walking in the wrong direction and abruptly turn around, forcing someone to quickly dodge out of your way, or worse, bump into you.

You will find yourself lost much less often if you buy a map of New York and tape it up somewhere in your apartment. Compared to most cities, Manhattan is actually quite sensibly organized along a grid, with the exception of famously labyrinthine neighborhoods like the West Village or the Financial District. Either navigate by landmarks, such as the Empire State Building or One World Trade Center, which can be seen from almost everywhere, or harness the power of the sun; since New York is north of the equator, the sun is always in the southern part of the sky, toward the east in the morning and the west in the afternoon. If that doesn't work, just walk a couple of blocks; you'll inevitably note the street numbers changing the right or wrong way, or you'll come across a major avenue you recognize.

Second, walk on the right—as far to the right as you can get without grinding into a building. As with other mighty rivers, New York traffic moves fastest in the middle and slowest at the edges. By walking at the margin of the crowd, you will also have access to plenty of places to step out of the flow: behind standpipes and street signs and into building alcoves and so on, should you need to stop and get your bearings. Keeping to the right is doubly important on escalators, stairs, and subway platforms—all places where a crowd is trying to squeeze through a narrow passage, and where, should you accidentally encumber traffic, you are likely to draw negative attention to yourself. And God help you if you inexplicably stop in front of the turnstiles when the train is pulling into the station.

Third, do not jaywalk until you've been here at least a year. Your brain has not yet learned to reliably calibrate the speeds of passing taxis, buses, and delivery bikers, and there is a good chance you'll screw it up and get run over. Yes, most New Yorkers will cross in the middle of the street, or at corners against the light when they sense that it is safe. They have already acquired this skill. Use your first months here to watch their movements and learn the timing—and when you begin to do likewise, stick to the side streets and quieter neighborhoods until you really get the hang of it. I'm pretty sure bad crossing is the leading cause of death in newly arrived New Yorkers! That, and ordering Papa John's. You live in the pizza capital of the world; what's wrong with you?

I also have a theory that much of New Yorkers' reputation for being rude stems from tourists' experience of our walking speed. They come to the city for a week, see the crowds rushing to and fro, maybe get jostled a few times, and come to the conclusion that New Yorkers are mean and dislike outsiders. Nothing could be further from the truth. Approached in the correct way, New Yorkers are some of the most helpful people on Earth, trained by a long history of helping immigrants and lost tourists get where they need to go.

What is the correct method of approach? First, spot a knowledgeable New Yorker—an easy way is to pick the person who seems most at ease, and who doesn't have any of the tell-tale signs of outsiders here: shorts of an awkward length, I Love New York gear, or any kind of fanny pack not, obviously, worn ironically. Second, approach them at a natural place of pause—while they're waiting for traffic to pass at a corner or on line at the halal cart. Third, ask your question in a clear, loud voice, and then listen carefully for the response because it will not be repeated.

You will find that the vast majority of New Yorkers are eager to show off their knowledge of the city. A personal example: For five years I lived in Brooklyn Heights, close to the Brooklyn Bridge. Almost every day on the way to work I'd find a group of lost tourists outside of the High Street station trying to figure out how to get to the Brooklyn Bridge steps, and nothing made me happier than successfully guiding them to their some-what-hidden destination under an overpass two blocks away. I did this nearly every day I lived there, and I still feel a certain glow when I reflect on the many confused visitors I was able to send on the right path.

One word of caution: It is often best, when getting directions, to ask two people, or to double check with your phone's map, because the local tendency to be helpful with directions sometimes conflicts with the fact that many New Yorkers have a fairly bad sense of direction outside the five blocks around their home or work. There is also a strong desire here not to look like a chump who doesn't know his way around, so rather than simply admit they don't know how to get to where you need to go, they'll just make an "educated" guess, and suddenly you're on a PATH train to Jersey City instead of a 7 train to Queens.

But sometimes New Yorkers don't even need to be asked to offer assistance. I'm not talking about times of emergency—hurricanes, terrorist attacks—when the local willingness to help ends up in the national news. I mean the little dramas you see all the time here, when someone faints on the subway and ten people immediately clear a bench and offer water, or a cyclist gets doored by a car and five bystanders rush in to make sure he's not too seriously injured and to call an ambulance.

Or how about this one: I was locking up my bike last week on Third Avenue and Twentieth Street, going to meet a friend, when suddenly, I saw a dog break its leash and run straight up the middle of Third Avenue with its owner screaming, running after it. Before I could even stand up, at least twenty ordinary New Yorkers dropped what they were doing and immediately began running after the dog. One second they had their typical implacable New York faces on, the next, they were flying up the street after a stranger's pet. I wasn't at all surprised—New Yorkers love to help people out.

A final thought: New Yorkers walk with speed and focus because otherwise they'd have a hard time getting anything done here. As you settle in, try to live all aspects of your life with a similar sense of purpose. In your first months you'll find New York presents you with endless distractions: bad tabloids that promote toxic values of wealth and fame, superficial careerists more interested in networking than friendship, overpriced trendy spots that just leave you feeling ripped off. Ignore as much of this stuff as you can. Pick your destination—fulfilling job, kind friends, stimulating art—and advance toward it, eyes always on the goal.

Also avoid any open manholes and rusted sidewalk cellar doors—those can really be killers.

Good luck!
Jake

Dear Jake,

When I lived in the Midwest and saw New Yorkers on TV shows, they were always so tough; you know, the gruff, no-nonsense guys you see on police shows. So I was kind of shocked, after I moved here, to find that almost all of my New York acquaintances complain constantly about their lives in the city. What's up with that?

Yours truly,
Stiff Upper Lip

Dear SUL,

Many things you learn about New York from television are wrong; for instance, the size of the typical New York apartment, the number of murders that take place in an average year, or the odds of acquaintances bumping into each other on the street every day—all three are grossly overstated on typical shows. So it's no surprise you got the wrong idea about how New Yorkers act. I know of no locals who embody the most common stereotypes—the New Yorker as stoic and sullen or loud-mouthed and sarcastic—though of course everyone I know here passes through these attitudes from time to time. I've also never seen anyone jump in a cab and scream, "Follow that car!"

Do real New Yorkers complain a lot? Yes, of course. They complain because living here is hard—physically, socially, emotionally—and despite its challenges, they want to stay, so what else is there to do besides let off some steam? Especially about things everyone can agree on: that the rent is too damn high, that whatever train you rely on takes forever, that car alarms were created by the devil to torture innocent people and have never once stopped a vehicle from being stolen. Without this type of therapeutic kvetching, who knows what number of senseless acts of violence would occur every day?

(For many New Yorkers, cursing is a similar means of harmlessly reducing tension. This sometimes shocks or frightens new arrivals who hail from places where "fuck" isn't used as a routine intensifier, as in the sentence "Look at this fucking line—there's no fucking way I'm waiting forty-five fucking minutes for a fucking burger with a fucking bun made out of fucking ramen.")

Whining about shared problems also creates an important sense of community here. This is important because, in a dense metropolis, it is critical to experience a sense of connection with others. Casual relationships with coworkers, neighbors, and social acquaintances are maintained and strengthened through the frequent rehashing of these common problems. People who suffer in silence miss out on this camaraderie and magnify their troubles.

Complaining serves another purpose, which is that it allows New Yorkers to identify where they fall in New York's complex web of class, race, and neighborhood identity. You can bet that the swells in Manhattan's more exclusive neighborhoods like Gramercy spend less time complaining about rent than working class families in Sunset Park do, but they spend a lot more time complaining about bike lanes and Citi Bike docks taking over their carefully cultivated streetscapes. By griping about the right mix of things, you show others here where you come from and where you belong.

Complaining about gentrification is a perfect example. Talk to any New Yorker who's been here longer than three years, and eventually the conversation will come around to what the city was like at some earlier time, and how much more real/better/cooler it was back then—even if back then was only eleven months ago. This type of complaining is a demonstration of a New Yorker's bona fides, a show of how real they are disguised as a little aria about how New York is always getting worse. Don't take it at face value.

Despite their income or race or location, there are some commonalities in New Yorkers' complaints. I've noticed we rarely gripe about topics that are really big or really small. For instance, no one ever seems to mention the threat of climate change or a terrorist attack when they're venting with friends. Existential risk is something we New Yorkers bring to our therapists but not to brunch. Same with stuff at the other end of the spectrum: piddling troubles, like a cockroach crawling through your hair in bed or stepping knee-deep in a corner slush lagoon in winter—those things seem to be taken in stride and treated as beneath our dignity to complain about.

When the really bad stuff happens—fires, explosions, blackouts, floods—you never hear New Yorkers complain. No one says, "Why us?" No, we just go right to work helping each other—calling on the rich social networks that all our daily bitching helped create. So, in a sense, I think the day-to-day gripe-a-thon is one of the secrets of New Yorkers' incredible resilience in times of adversity. Also, you try being a Mets fan.

Here is my advice: join in. Find a group of friends, get comfortable, and then tell them everything about this place that's driving you crazy. It's better to get it out in an understanding environment, rather than save it all up and explode one day on the subway platform.

In solidarity,
Jake

N.B.: Some of New York complaining has cultural roots in our various ethnic traditions. My people, the Jews, have a rich history of complaining that has woven its way into the typical New York attitude. It can be summarized by this classic joke: A Jewish grandmother is watching her grandson play on the beach when a huge wave arrives and pulls him out to sea. She prays, "Please God, save my only grandchild. I beg of you, please bring him back!" Suddenly, another big wave comes and throws the boy back onto the beach, unharmed. She looks up toward heaven and says, "He had a hat!"

Dear Jake,

Ever since I moved to Bed-Stuy in Brooklyn, I've really been feeling paranoid about safety. I'm a white 22-year-old woman, and even though I know the neighborhood has gotten much safer recently, and my block seems fine, I've been feeling worried about coming back from places late at night because it's a five-block walk from the train. Is this all in my head? Do natives worry about crime? How can I avoid being the transplant who gets mugged or stabbed or worse?

Sincerely,
Scared of Everything

Dear SOE,

Don't apologize for feeling scared; that's a perfectly normal reaction for a person to have when they move someplace new and are just getting to know their way around. Fear is our bodies' natural way of keeping us from doing stupid shit, like walking with headphones on at night down poorly lit blocks or leaving windows unlocked when we leave for work. Listen to the fear—it's often a good teacher—but do not let yourself be carried away by it. As you said, New York has become a very safe city, and by adopting just a few street-smart native customs, you will likely avoid any trouble for as long as you live here.

However, this was not always so! When I was growing up in the city in the late 1980s, crime was about five times worse than it is today. According to the official NYPD stats, in 1990 there were 2,262 murders and 527,257 serious crimes versus the 352 murders and 105,456 serious crimes in 2015. I remember, when I was first commuting to school in Manhattan as a little thirteen-year-old in 1989, it was like I had a sign on my back that said, "PLEASE ROB ME!" Coming into the city in the morning, I was robbed for wristwatches until I stopped wearing them. Coming home, I was taken for my lunch money or my backpack or even, once, for the slice of pizza I was literally about to bite into. I was mugged by teenagers and adults on subway trains, subway platforms, and sidewalks, mostly with knives or box cutters, but at least once with a gun.

This period lasted about two years, until I had grown a lot taller and there were younger kids who were easier to victimize than me. But during that time, I developed a wonderfully acute sense for danger. For instance, I knew that taking the F home was a bad idea from 3 p.m. to 5 p.m. during the week, because roughneck teens were getting out of school and liable to get on at half a dozen stops between the Village and Park Slope. So I'd wait until five, when the rush-hour crowds started, and usually found safety in numbers.

I also learned to read people: the subtle body language tics people give off when they're looking for trouble, those side glances and whispers to their accomplices. Also, how to tell the difference between someone who's actually out to do you harm and someone who's just harmlessly screaming at strangers—a lot of New York street smarts comes down to being able to separate the real threats from the empty ones. You don't want to freak out every time someone acts a little weird here, because in New York, that's going to happen about five times a day.

Allow me to offer some practical advice born out of my experiences in the bad old days. The key to safety is, of course, awareness of your surroundings. That means silencing your headphones, earbuds, etc., to hear what's going on around you. It means being present and noticing when someone or something feels out of place. New Yorkers who have been here a while have a way of always glancing around, taking in the scene. There's a persistently wrong notion among tourists that New Yorkers never make eye contact with strangers. Quite the opposite—we make brief eye contact all the time as we survey our surroundings.

For this reason, we are rarely surprised, and this sends a subtle signal to potential predators that we're not going to be an easy target and they should probably just move on. You'll encourage this by looking and acting like you belong exactly where you are. That goes for everything from the way you stand (back straight, with confidence), to the way you walk (fast, like you know where you're going), to how you dress (inconspicuously, in typically muted New York colors, with a minimum of flashy jewelry and accessories).

This advice goes double, unfortunately, for women, who, whether because of their smaller size or because they carry their money in more easily accessible purses, generally tend to be more attractive prey for criminals. Almost all of the women I know carry their purses cross shoulder on the subway, and they never, ever, leave them hanging over a chair at restaurants. They are also generally more clued into potential threats than men, having been raised in a society where cat-calling, groping, and worse are all-too-frequent phenomena.

What happens if these preemptive tactics aren't enough and you become one of the few people who get mugged in present-day New York City? Take this advice, given by every New York parent to their kid sometime before they get their first MetroCard: "Just hand it over." Every single time I got jumped when I was younger, that approach saved my skin, and it will save yours. The question is what, exactly, you're handing over. A native custom in the '80s was to always have some "mugger money" ready and separate from your wallet for times of need. If you do have to give up your wallet, you will feel better about the transaction if you made a list of all the cards inside and left the list somewhere safe at home.

If, and this is really so unlikely it hardly bears mentioning in a city where the most dangerous neighborhoods are now as safe as the Upper East Side was when I was a kid, you encounter someone who wants to actually do you physical harm—a rapist or stabber or whacked-out crazy person high on bath salts—what should you do? Unfortunately, you will probably be unarmed. Back in the day, carrying a screwdriver, pepper spray, or brass knuckles was considered every New Yorker's God-given right, but years of decreasing crime combined with the heavy use of stop-and-frisk tactics by the police during the 2000s has made carrying self-defense weapons decidedly not worth the risk for most people.

However, not carrying a weapon doesn't necessarily mean you're defenseless. Keys, properly positioned between your fingers, are surprisingly effective for slashing attackers, as are a swift kick to the crotch or punch to the neck. Taking a self-defense course will make these moves automatic and raise your confidence. I'll always remember the advice of my karate teacher down at the local YMCA: "Jake," he said, "in New York there's no such thing as fighting dirty. Go for the eyes." He also recommended screaming "fire" rather than "help," because he said jaded New Yorkers might ignore the latter but never the former.

Obviously, once the danger, whatever it is, has passed, you should call 911. Given the relative rarity of muggings and assaults in New York these days, you can expect the NYPD to arrive quickly. They may even take you for a ride around the neighborhood looking for the assailant— quite a few muggers have been caught this way, especially if they're dumb enough to grab a phone that broadcasts its location. You will be more helpful to the police if you've made an effort to remember exactly what your assailants were wearing, what they looked like, and in which direction they ran.

There is a bright side to getting robbed: This is a real New York experience that few people get to have these days, and you'll be able to lord the story over your friends for years as a sign of your authenticity. Or, if you're too mature for that, you can simply use the occasion to meditate on the uncertainty of life, the relative lack of value material things have when compared to your health, and feel thankful.

Again, it's unlikely that you will ever be mugged, manhandled, or assaulted during the years you live in New York. Statistically speaking, most crime victims know their assailants, and stranger-on-stranger crime is a very small percentage of our currently historically low crime numbers. Your anxiety should be proportional to the actual danger, which, in this case, is small. Once you've lived in your new neighborhood for a while, have gotten to know your neighbors and local shopkeepers, and learned the rhythms of the local streets, you'll probably find that your acute worry recedes to a normal level of New York vigilance.

That said, do your best to avoid looking like an easy target staggering home drunk at three in the morning (suck it up and get in a cab). If you have a bedroom window that opens onto a fire escape, keep it locked. And if you find yourself walking toward a group or individual who seems menacing, for whatever reason, give yourself permission to simply cross the street.

If your anxieties continue, investigate whether there are other causes. Could it be connected to being a white woman in a neighborhood that is still predominantly black? Is it because of some past trauma you haven't dealt with, but should? Are you consuming bad media—tabloid newspapers, for instance—that overcover crime because they know it sells copies and encourages people to fear minorities and poor people? Which serves the political interests of their rich owners? You must think carefully and find the real root of your problem.

While you do that, I recommend thinking about this: The very small risk of crime is a small price to pay for living in the greatest city on Earth. What's more, there are worse things than being forced to live in the moment with an awareness of your surroundings—many people pay for meditation classes designed to produce the same experience—and here you are getting it for free just by walking down a New York street at night!

Namaste,
Jake

N.B.: We tend to be frightened of the unknown. If you are afraid of your new neighborhood, take steps to get to know it better. Participate in your community, join the block association (or start one if it doesn't exist!). Find out when and where your local community board meets and attend a meeting—if safety is your biggest concern, attend on one of the nights when the local NYPD precinct captain appears to answer questions. You could also consider getting involved with other community groups, like the Coalition for the Improvement of Bedford-Stuyvesant.

Dear Jake,

I was out for drinks last night with two of my friends, both of whom have lived here a lot longer than I have. After three beers, they got into an increasingly heated argument over where to find the best pizza in New York that literally ended with one of them storming off to "smoke a cigarette" and not coming back to the table. Their basic disagreement was over some dumb aspect of pizza preparation— like, how thick the crust is supposed to be, whether the cheese is supposed to be uniform across the top or in little glops. Like any sane person, I don't really care about this stuff, but it did make me wonder: Why do New Yorkers always have to be right about everything? Why can't people here let anything go?

Sincerely,
Puzzled by Pizza Persistency

———————

Dear PBPP,

Pizza, to a real New Yorker, is no trivial matter. It is not only a major source of sustenance here, but it is also an important source of civic pride. I'd go so far as to say that if you don't have an opinion about where to get the best pizza, you haven't lived here long enough. So, when you hear your friends arguing over whether the best is Grimaldi's thin crust with pieces of fresh mozzarella, or a slightly thicker-bodied slice with a full-cheese covering like you find at Joe's Pizza, don't roll your eyes: They're trying to communicate deeply held beliefs about this city that may be about more than food.

For instance, imagine one New Yorker making the argument that the best pizza in the city is the Axl Rosenberg pie at noted hipster spot Roberta's (sopressata, double garlic, jalapeno, and mushroom). Your other friend screams, "That's not fucking pizza—that's performance art." Obviously, they're not just disagreeing about the merits of pizza toppings. One is asserting a certain position about New York: That its essence is innovation and experimentation. The other is taking the traditionalist position, which is that pizza, like all other things about New York, achieved perfection years ago and it shouldn't be meddled with or changed.

It's easy to miss these nuances when your friends argue like real New Yorkers, what with all the gesticulating and the shouting and the "You have NO clue what you're talking about!" For the first years you're here, this local conversational style will seem overbearing, and you may feel it's impossible to get a word in edgewise. But it's like stepping onto a really crowded train: A tourist is going to say there's no way in and just wait for another opportunity that may never come, but a lifer is going to find a way to weasel on, even if it means cramming himself between a pregnant woman and a guy on crutches and getting yelled at. What I'm saying is that you will get the hang of it, and as your own volume increases, you'll be able to focus more on the content of the argument and less on the theatrics.

It's not all theatrics, of course. New Yorkers really do care passionately about details of city life that might seem insignificant to outsiders—not just about the best food or the best restaurants or bars—but about the best neighborhood to live in, or even the best park. We must recognize that there are positive aspects to this New York attitude: It encourages a strong connection to the city because every opinion is stated with the conviction that people elsewhere reserve for religious beliefs, and it is often genuinely edifying to newcomers like yourself who might not actually know a lot about important things like where to buy the best knish (obviously Yonah Schimmel's on Houston).

New York stubbornness isn't always for the best, of course; sometimes it's a sign of defensiveness and insecurity. About what? All New Yorkers, even the natives, have at least once woken up in the middle of the night with that "oh fuck" feeling that living here is just insane and unhealthy and they've got to get out. As we've discussed, there are many reasons, material and spiritual, why this feeling is baseless and must be ignored, but the feeling still occasionally asserts itself and, from time to time, it must be dispelled like lancing a boil.

Sometimes this comes by arguing with outsiders; explaining why, on any given metric, the city is superior to the one they come from (sometimes people actually do this in book form!). Even when this seems nonsensical—say, arguing with someone from San Francisco that our burritos are better—we can't help ourselves, and we will find some example, however minute, to justify our position: "I'm sure you think that burrito you get in the Mission is the best, but it's just because you've never been to Taqueria Tlaxcalli in Parkchester and tried the steamed tongue—it makes the ones in San Francisco taste like dog food wrapped in newspaper!"

This, of course, is immature, and the more you do it, the more you betray the weakness of your commitment to New York. An insecure resident may, when confronted by the tomato casserole that his Chicago acquaintance presents as pizza, embark on a lengthy diatribe along the lines of "What the fuck is this garbage?" Whereas a wise native is more likely to just give a slight smirk and say something like "I've never tried pizza-flavored soup!"

Restraining yourself from correcting others on minor New York matters is likewise difficult—as when your visiting relatives pronounce Houston Street like the city in Texas, or say they're going to stand *in* line at TKTS, the discount-ticket stand in Times Square. If you can resist shouting, "It's How-ston!" or "In New York we say '*on* line,'" you have progressed far down the road to maturity.

It's even worse when New Yorkers vent their insecurities at each other. Although, like complaining, arguing over things like which baseball team is best does release some tension and lubricate social interactions; when taken to an extreme, you get nothing but hurt feelings and occasional fistfights. This is particularly true of one no-win argument that comes up all the time: Which neighborhood or borough is best?

All New Yorkers, except those who are forced by fate to live there, will agree that Times Square is a maddeningly overcrowded tourist trap to be avoided at all cost, but it's so much easier to agree on what's the worst than on what is the best. Even people from superficially similar neighborhoods, say Park Slope and the Upper West Side, or from conjoined boroughs, like Brooklyn and Queens, will argue from now until dooms-day about why one place is the best and the other is the worst.

This is because the idea that there might be a better mode of living, right here in the city, is intolerable to us. Our New York must be the best New York, the most authentic, the one with the most heart. The extent to which New Yorkers are judgmental toward each other stems from this: The terror of knowing that someone else has found a better way to live here than we have, and that our suffering—even the smallest part of our suffering here—has been wasted.

So, the next time you see two New Yorkers getting into a fight about some stupid shit, have sympathy. Know they are dealing with great exis-tential stress in the only way they know how. Instead of judging them, play the peacemaker and say, "Guys, I don't know which one of you is right, but I think you can both agree that even the worst slice of pizza here is better than the best one you can get in Philadelphia."

Or, I don't know, perhaps you could suggest they go out for Korean BBQ instead?

Sincerely,
Jake

Ten Things All Native New Yorkers Carry Around

1 **METROCARD.** Who has money for cabs when the rent is so damn high? Anyway, the subway is usually faster. Usually.

2 **CITI BIKE FOB.** For use when the subway isn't faster because the state has failed to adequately invest in infrastructure.

3 **A BOOK.** Most New Yorkers don't drive, so there's more opportunity to read. And you never know when you're going to have a few minutes of downtime, whether it's on the subway, on the bus, or at a local bar while waiting for your phone to charge.

4 **EARBUDS.** For drowning out crazy people screaming in your subway car.

5 **SUNGLASSES.** For avoiding eye contact, especially with coworkers you see on the subway.

6 **HAND SANITIZER.** In case you touched anything on the subway.

7 **AT LEAST TWENTY DOLLARS IN CASH.** You're not using a credit card at a bodega to buy gum.

8 **IDNYC CARD.** This gets you free entrance into almost every museum in town; it's also a convenient ID for police when you get busted riding your Citi Bike on a sidewalk because you're trying to avoid getting killed by NYC drivers.

9 **KEYS.** For unlocking doors, like your house or the office building you used to work in but whose bathroom you still use because it's the only clean one in Midtown; also for self-defense and opening Amazon boxes.

10 **AN EXPANSIVE SENSE OF PERSONAL SPACE.** Take a step back, tourists.

Hi Jake,

The other day I was coming home from work on the 6 train. It was a completely normal commute until just after Times Square, when I looked up, and directly across from me was a guy with a large white rat on his shoulder. He looked me right in the eyes and placed the rat headfirst into his mouth. The rat kind of shook its butt back and forth for, like, ten seconds, and then he took it out of his mouth, placed it back on his shoulder, looked at me again, and took out his phone and started playing a game. While this was going on, literally not a single person seated around me seemed to even notice—like, they clearly saw what he was doing, but it was like they thought, "Oh, just another guy with a rat in his mouth," like that happens every day on their commute. How did New Yorkers become so accepting of crazy stuff like this?

Sincerely,
Rattled

Dear Rattled,

I think I've seen this guy around, too; sometimes the rats are dyed other colors, like bright blue or red. He's actually just one of several animal eccentrics you see sometimes on the train here. I can think of at least two snake charmers and one imposing gentleman with a colorful parrot. Some are actually commuting from SoHo or Times Square where they pose with tourists for tips. Others are strictly amateur, and I think they enjoy the reactions they get from new arrivals like you as a kind of hobby or fetish.

You observed that New Yorkers are "accepting" of this kind of thing, but I think acceptance is the wrong word here. That would imply we've thought deeply about whatever weirdness has been placed in front of us, and we have decided that we approve of it. Quite the contrary! If we really gave a lot of thought to every strange thing we saw on the 6 train—a guy transporting an upright piano, a woman eating a sushi platter on a folding table, teenage acrobats kicking their feet inches from our nose—we wouldn't have time to think about anything else, like how late we are to work, or why we keep paying thirteen dollars for a salad at lunch.

No, what you witnessed wasn't acceptance but tolerance, which is when a New Yorker decides that whatever insane shit is going on simply doesn't annoy us enough to do something about it. Monkey wearing a diaper sitting on a bench on the F train? No problem. Monkey wearing a diaper sitting on a bench on the F train AND taking up two seats? Absolutely not—it's one seat per primate, and that monkey is definitely going to get yelled at by someone.

The key distinction is whether the weirdness in question is harming anyone. We don't give a flying fuck about violations of social mores that would drive more conservative Americans insane. The whole idea of the "judgmental New Yorker" who dresses all in black and demands others do the same is a tedious stereotype spread by lazy writers and directors who've never really *lived* in New York City.

New York is without question the best place in the world to be a misfit. If you've been cast out by some small-minded little town somewhere for being different—gay, trans, goth, too intellectual, too into fashion, a member of some persecuted minority or religious group—you know you'll find a home here, and a community of hundreds or thousands of people who came here for the same reason. This is why New York is always ahead of the curve on every civil rights movement, and why so many great advancements, like the fight for LGBTQ rights, began here.

This tolerance has been part of the city's DNA since the Dutch settled here in 1624. These original colonists came to the new world to trade, and that meant throwing the doors wide open to anyone with money to spend or goods to sell. Contrast this with the English colonies, which were set up by fundamentalist pilgrims fleeing religious persecution. They brought with them a very strict set of rules for how people should live their lives, and they also brought a tendency to stone or hang anyone who violated them. Four hundred years later, cities like Boston and Philadelphia still have this small-minded "our way or the highway" air about them, while New York has become a world city open to all.

You see this even in our most parochial quarters; think about neighborhoods far from Manhattan that are typically considered inward-looking. For example, on Arthur Avenue, long an Italian stronghold, most of the Italian places are now run by Albanians. And if you prefer to eat Mexican or Chinese food, you don't even have to leave the main strip. Sunset Park used to be known as Little Norway and Finn Town, but it's been Brooklyn's Chinatown for at least twenty-five years. What I'm saying is there's almost no neighborhood, anywhere in the city, that's truly insular and closed to outsiders (the few exceptions being Orthodox Jewish neighborhoods in Williamsburg, Crown Heights, and Bensonhurst). Decades of gentrification and immigration have brought diversity to just about every corner of the city.

This does not mean each of our ethnic groups has always gotten along. Tolerance is a fragile thing, and waves of immigration usually pitted the new arrivals against those who came before in a fight over the worst jobs and housing. This has led periodically to outbreaks of violence—for instance, the Draft Riots of 1863, the Harlem Riots of 1943 and '64, or the Crown Heights Riots of 1991. On the whole, however, tolerance has ultimately won out over divisiveness.

Did you know New Yorkers have one of the highest rates of passport possession in the entire United States? Some of this is because we are a city composed of immigrants; more than a third of city residents were born in another country. But even lifelong New Yorkers remain fundamentally interested in the outside world. Yes, of course, we still believe that New York is the greatest place in the world to live, but this belief is not based on willful ignorance of other places. In fact, it's the opposite: We know New York is the greatest place to live because we've traveled outside the city, and we've welcomed the best parts of the world back into New York.

The only thing I can definitively say New Yorkers are intolerant of is intolerance itself. Apart from small redoubts of conservatism, for instance in Staten Island or on the Upper East Side, the city is incredibly progressive, and it is at least twenty years ahead of the rest of the country on most social issues. This can sometimes lead to unpleasant conflicts when we visit with relatives who live back in the rest of America; rather than feel a quiet pride in the moral progress we've made, New Yorkers sometimes feel the urge to condescendingly lecture the residents of less forward-thinking places about their intolerance—be it racism, sexism, nationalism, or whatever.

This is, of course, a terrible way to win anyone over to our way of thinking, and it only further cements our reputation for being judgmental assholes. If you ever find yourself in such a situation, try to remember that what makes our city great is the relaxed openness of our tolerance, the live-and-let-live attitude that lets so many small provocations and annoyances just wash right over us without getting us bent out of shape. Now apply that same feeling to your conservative brother-in-law at Thanksgiving dinner, or your uncle who won't stop asking how you can live in a Sodom-and-Gomorrah-ish place like New York.

If you can deal with stuff like that without losing your cool, you're truly starting to become one of us. Good work!

To a kinder world,
Jake

N.B.: The wise native knows that just as there is no light without darkness, and no falafel platter without tahini, there can be no New York without places outside it. It's only in relation to the suburbs or the Midwest or California that the true virtues of this place get thrown into high relief, and for that alone we should value them.

New York now leads the world's greatest cities in the number of people around whom you shouldn't make a sudden move.

—DAVID LETTERMAN

CHAPTER 3

How to Keep a Roof Over Your Head

Questions

New York City is a great
monument to the power
of money and greed . . .
a race for rent.

—FRANK LLOYD WRIGHT

Dear Jake,

I moved to New York over the summer, and I'm doing pretty well: I found two part-time gigs (one waitressing, one bartending), and a two-day-a-week internship at a fashion label, which is my dream job. Only one problem: I've got to find a place to live. So far, I've survived by cat sitting for a friend who was out of town, but she's coming back and there's literally no room in her tiny East Village studio for two people. I've been spending all of my free time scanning craigslist, but there aren't any apartments I can afford alone, and all the roommate-wanted listings are way out in Brooklyn or Queens, and I hardly even know my way around Manhattan. What should I do? Where does someone just starting out here find an apartment they can afford?

Sincerely,
Hunting and Hating It

Dear HAHI,

Congratulations on a successful arrival in this fine city. A lot of young people make the mistake of trying to find a job and apartment all at the same time, which is a recipe for going insane. You've followed a smarter path: Finding some temporary housing with friends, relatives, or a cheap sublet, then securing some remunerative employment that will provide the cash you need to go apartment hunting in New York.

It's called apartment *hunting* for a reason. A good, cheap place in a convenient location is elusive prey indeed. Like Bigfoot or the Loch Ness monster, these apartments are far more often seen in television shows and movies than in real life. Picture Monica's two-bedroom apartment (with a balcony!) in the West Village on *Friends,* which she conveniently inherited from her grandmother and appeared to pay almost nothing for; or Carrie Bradshaw's one-bedroom apartment on the Upper East Side (with a walk-in closet!), which she somehow paid for with a freelance writing gig. Many young people have been cruelly misled by these fictions, and they end up depressed when they discover the reality of New York City housing.

So a brief review of the basics for those people who haven't yet begun the search: New York is one of the most expensive housing markets in the world, with vacancy levels routinely below 3 percent, which means any decent apartment that does become available will be more expensive than you can afford and immediately fought over by dozens of anxious house hunters. Picture malnourished, rabid hyenas tearing apart a zebra foal, multiply that savagery by ten, and you're still not close to the kind of frenzy New Yorkers are driven to when seeking shelter.

What's worse, New York's byzantine housing laws mean that the market is actually bifurcated into two different pools of apartments: rent-stabilized places for longtime residents, with affordable, regulated rents, and intensely overpriced "luxury" market–rate housing for new arrivals like you. You will understand and appreciate these laws eventually if you stay here for a long time, but at the beginning of your New York journey, you will find that they only make the search more difficult.

So what to do? You have already sussed out that Manhattan is basically a red zone, with almost no apartments affordable to young people outside some shrinking redoubts far north in Inwood and Washington Heights, or in East Harlem. Living anywhere south of Central Park is difficult indeed. Some will find success by going far east, to Kips Bay or Murray Hill, but even there the pickings are slim, and even people with Wall Street–trainee gigs find themselves bunking up two and three to an apartment. What's worse, these neighborhoods have little to show in terms of good restaurants and bars, and you're going to find yourself spending a lot of time commuting to more convivial destinations in Brooklyn and Queens for fun.

For the past five or ten years, my younger friends have looked over this landscape and quickly beaten a path toward the outer boroughs. When asked for advice, I, a native of South Brooklyn, recommend the more affordable, youth-friendly neighborhoods along the A/C trains:

Clinton Hill, Crown Heights, Bed-Stuy. As time has passed, and these neighborhoods have gotten less affordable, my friends have been moving farther east and south—some have reached East New York, and the rest have looked on the N/R subway lines in Sunset Park and Bay Ridge. The same process has been going on in northern Brooklyn along the L line: Twenty years ago, young people were renting in Williamsburg, ten years ago in Bushwick, and now in Ridgewood (which is actually in Queens—although many would say that if you're considering Queens, you'd do better to look along the 7 train in Sunnyside, Woodside, or Jackson Heights, as Ridgewood is less convenient than those areas. Neighborhoods like Astoria and Long Island City have been overpriced for several years.)

Some people will say that Brooklyn and Queens have already gotten so hot that it's impossible to find an affordable place in either and you should consider the South Bronx, which is only twenty minutes to Midtown on the 4/5 subway and considerably safer than most people believe, with prices that are still reasonable. I also have one friend who grew up on Staten Island who vehemently argues that St. George and the surrounding neighborhoods by the ferry are undiscovered gems where, if you don't mind a boat commute (which is free!), you can find one-bedroom apartments for $1,500. The point is that in all five boroughs, there are still pockets of affordability if you're prepared to compromise.

Compromise on what, exactly? First, space: The less you need, the less you'll pay. This shouldn't be a big deal, because if your priority was a spacious house and a backyard, you'd still be living in the suburbs. Second, privacy: Splitting any apartment with a roommate (or better yet, boyfriend or girlfriend) is the quickest way to reduce your rent to an affordable amount. You'd be surprised at how many one-bedrooms can be converted to a small two-bedroom apartment with a simple pressure wall or set of tall bookcases. Third, distance to the subway: If you're willing to walk an extra five blocks, you will find many more apartments in your price range, and you will be surprised at how much more fit you become just getting to and from work.

When I graduated from college around the turn of the millennium, things were a little easier—the push to the outer boroughs was already in full swing, but there were still deals in the East Village and the Lower East Side if you were willing to look hard enough. My first apartment was on Orchard Street near Grand. A friend's cousin had already rented it when his roommate unexpectedly ran out of money and scrammed for the Midwest, so I took over his room. This was back in 2000, and we were the first gentrifiers in an old Chinese tenement, paying $1,900 a month for a tiny two-bedroom apartment where most of the rooms looked out onto an airshaft. Our new neighbors did not appreciate our presence: There was a small tar-covered roof accessible from the kitchen that we sometimes used as a place to sit outside, and when we did, they'd occasionally throw lit cigarettes and garbage out of their windows right down on us.

That's about par for the course. As we'll discuss later in this chapter, young people are unfortunately put in the position of being foot soldiers of gentrification, and this often creates conflicts with longtime residents of the neighborhood. That wasn't the only problem; like most of our friends, we were vastly overpaying for a crappy apartment in a neighborhood some people were still scared to explore at night. But you know what? It was great. I loved walking those streets, and I loved the feeling of having my own place, even though my bedroom wasn't much bigger than my single bed, and the bars on the window were so thick that hardly any light came through.

That's because I was finally living on my own in New York, and nothing else—not the location, not the size of the apartment, not my increasingly angry roommate (more on that later!)—could change or dampen that exhilarating feeling of freedom and possibility. You will have this experience, too—I guarantee it—no matter what neighborhood you end up in. In fact, the weirder and more unexpected the neighborhood you end up in, and the stranger your roommates, the more you'll feel it. That's because the point of moving to New York and finding your place in it is to expose you to the unknown and to people and situations you didn't expect. Facing the discomfort and adapting to it is the goal.

Some people come here and ask themselves "Which neighborhood best reflects the person I think I am and the life I want to live?" and then try to find that place, and because of the factors we've discussed, they end up disappointed when they find such a neighborhood or apartment doesn't exist or they can't afford it. You should take the opposite approach: Recognize that you're too young to have figured yourself out yet, and let New York answer that question for you. Pick the subway line that gets you closest to your job(s), trace it out to the first stop you might be able to afford, and start canvassing. Sure, hit craigslist and other websites, but also walk the streets. See if there are any local non-chain real estate brokers (they always seem to have the best leads) or buildings with for-rent signs and ask in the local coffee shop and bodega if anyone has any leads.

I think you'll soon find you're on your way—probably to the first of a series of imperfect living situations, but also to a real New York life of adventure.

Good luck!
Jake

N.B.: The best network in NYC for finding apartments isn't the internet— it's the friend-of-a-friend system. Tell *everyone* you meet that you're looking—you'll be surprised about how often a coworker turns out to need a roommate or has an acquaintance who she thinks you'll like who also needs a place. I know a guy who was desperate for a new apartment and was willing to share with total strangers. He printed out a bunch of amusing calling cards with his details and what he was looking for, and he handed them out to people at parties and bars. In this way, he found an apartment *and* a girlfriend in less than two weeks.

Ten Things Found in All Native New Yorkers' Apartments

1 Note on the front window to leave packages at the bodega—because otherwise the neighborhood kleptos are getting your vitamin delivery.

2 Ten or twenty umbrellas in various stages of disintegration—because you never have one when it starts raining, and you have to buy another from the extortionate umbrella vendors who seem to somehow only appear when it rains and then charge you ten dollars for one that breaks if someone breathes on it wrong.

3 Plungers, Drano, and possibly a twenty-five-foot drain snake. Our pipes are 100 years old and can be clogged by one square of toilet paper.

4 An entire cabinet filled with takeout containers, which are used as dishes, cups, and places to gather loose change.

5 Ten jackets in a pile on hooks by the door, out of which you're 100 percent guaranteed to select the wrong one for the prevailing weather.

6 A drawer full of takeout menus because it's still faster to use them than Seamless.

7 A baseball bat that you bought that one time an apartment was broken into on your block but that you now use mostly for killing roaches in difficult-to-reach spots.

8 An air conditioner, a fan, a white-noise machine, and several large pillows for the two nights a week garbage trucks come crashing down the street at 3 A.M.

9 About a hundred books and back issues of the *New Yorker*, piling up faster than your ability to read them.

10 A letter from your landlord informing you of their plan to evict you so they can use your apartment as an Airbnb for German tourists.

Dear Jake,

I've been trying to rent an apartment for the last couple of weeks, and I finally found a one-bedroom in Bushwick I can afford (with a roommate). We found it through a broker, but last night I was looking up the building and I discovered they do no-fee rentals through their own office. Can I legally and morally refuse to pay the broker and just deal directly with the landlord? We're staring down $4,000 in brokers' fees!

Sincerely,
Feeling Grifted

———————————

Dear FG,

New York tap water is very clean, but as you've discovered, we still have our fair share of parasites here. Real estate brokers are the ones who you will deal with most frequently, as they attempt to skim 15 percent of a year's rent every time you move. They exist as a consequence of our city's terminally messed-up shortage of affordable housing, they provide relatively little in the way of services to justify their costs, and yet they have managed to persist for decades with no signs of vanishing any time soon.

Why does renting an apartment in NYC require paying such an excessive fee, when in most other cities you can rent directly from a landlord with no fee, or where the landlord actually pays the broker's fee? If you ask the brokers, they'll say you're paying for a valuable service: access to apartments that aren't advertised on craigslist, help negotiating the rent, assistance organizing and filling out the rental documents, and a guarantee that you're not getting scammed.

As you've already learned, most of this is bullshit. Sure, there may be some apartments that a broker has exclusively, but those arrangements tend to be rare, especially at the lower-price points. That's why you see so many brokers posting duplicate ads for the same apartment each day on craigslist: The landlord (or the landlord's broker, who will claim half of that 15 percent fee) is willing to work with any broker who can bring in a client. Same goes for the other stuff—the price will either not be negotiable, or you would have been able to negotiate the same discount yourself; the "help" you get filling out the forms consists of being handed the forms by the broker and being told to fill them out; and sometimes, as in this case, it's actually the broker who is perpetrating the scam.

Do you have to pay a broker 15 percent for a no-fee apartment that he falsely advertised? Legally, no—assuming you have not signed a contract with the broker (which is why you never sign anything until you're absolutely certain you're going to take the place). Morally, absolutely not! He was showing you an apartment you could have gotten yourself, and even if he did you a small service by making you aware of the apartment, that service is certainly not worth $4,000. That doesn't mean he won't try to threaten, cajole, or sue you in small-claims court if you do go behind his back and take the place. Stories of shady brokers trying to intimidate clients (and occasionally gluing their locks) are legion in this town, so you might want to consider letting this apartment go and renting another no-fee place from the same landlord. They may have multiple units available.

To be sure, there are a few legitimate rental scams a broker may protect you from. The most common is a grifter who obtains keys to an empty apartment, advertises it for rent, and collects "security deposits" without actually having the right to rent it. You can generally avoid these through normal New York street smarts: not paying until you've actually seen the apartment and gotten a copy of the lease, never paying cash, and conducting a basic internet search about the building, landlord, and management company to make sure that they are who they say they are.

So, why, if brokers don't provide much in the way of benefit, do they still exist? The answer is simple supply and demand. In New York, the market for decent, affordable apartments is so tight that most renters will fork over the broker's fee out of sheer desperation to get the process over with. This suits the landlords fine because, unlike in other cities, they don't get stuck paying the broker themselves, and they get to avoid the hassle of screening applicants and showing the apartment.

So the status quo continues. The internet is generally good at fixing situations like this, in which consumers are getting skinned by middlemen, but so far, most of the innovation online has been in services like craigslist, Zillow, StreetEasy, and Trulia, which really function more as advertising tools for real estate brokers than as services to cut out the middlemen and allow renters to contract directly with the landlords. Still, almost all of them do have no-fee sections where the larger landlords advertise their units, and it's worth taking a few minutes to at least see what's available.

Will these apartments actually end up being cheaper than going through a broker? Maybe not—no-fee apartments are often found in larger, "luxury" buildings, and the landlord may use the no fee as an excuse to exact a higher monthly rent from you. It is sometimes the case that renting a cheaper apartment through a broker will actually work out better in the long run, and this is especially true if you can get the broker to discount her fee by threatening to take your business elsewhere. Note: Getting a discount is rare, and this will only work as a negotiation technique if you actually do have other options, so it often pays to work with a couple of brokers, or to tell the broker you have a no-fee option, so she knows that you're not just bluffing.

Though it may be difficult, try to have some compassion for the broker. Most are not grifters, and they often have to hustle an enormous amount just to make not-great wages. Some are getting paid only on commission, and they don't even clear enough to afford their own rent some months, even while spending their days dealing with sleazy landlords and anxious, vacillating renters. If you do find one you like to work with, who actually does have some apartments you haven't already seen online, and who is honest and diligent, maybe you won't mind the 15 percent so much, especially when you realize your broker's portion of the fee is probably only half that (the rest goes to his employer).

If, however, you really can't stand to work with middlemen, and you've found the no-fee searches online haven't produced much, I do have one final suggestion: Hit the streets. Ask your friends if they've heard of any apartments in their buildings coming on the market, and talk to the supers or front-desk guys at the larger buildings. I know many people who stumbled into reasonably priced apartments this way, and they often avoided the broker's fee by connecting directly with a landlord.

Perhaps one day, in the far future, when the city has built more housing and the internet has fully automated the application process and created a real multiple-listings service showing all available apartments, this won't be quite so difficult. Until then, it's every man for himself, and you will probably end up paying one way or another—either with money to a broker, or with hours of your time, or both. Try to think of it as part of your long-term admission price to the greatest city in the world. There's a reason why it's so easy to find a spacious two-bedroom apartment up in Albany.

Sincerely,
Jake

N.B.: Once you're in an apartment and have been there awhile, always check with New York's Division of Housing and Community Renewal, which can tell you if your apartment is rent-stabilized and if it's being rented at the correct rent. I have plenty of acquaintances who have discovered their landlords were wildly overcharging them, and a few of them even won substantial refunds after consulting a lawyer.

Dear Jake,

I recently moved in with one of my friends from college. We had been pretty close but never lived together before we graduated and got to New York six months ago. Unfortunately, he's turned out to be a roommate from hell. He never cleans up—dirty dishes in the sink; living room constantly trashed—and he monopolizes the TV almost every night because his girlfriend is always over and they watch whatever they want, with no regard for me. The apartment is the size of a postage stamp and the walls are made of some kind of likely flammable cardboard, so I can hear everything (and I mean *everything*) those two are doing. All the time.

I've dropped a few hints about whether they could spend more time at her place, or if they could at least clean up after themselves, but so far I've gotten nowhere. I'm really getting frustrated: I'm busting my ass to pay for this place, and I don't want to have to act like their butler as well. What can I do to improve this situation?

Sincerely,
Really Hating Roommate

Dear RHR,

You have my sympathy! Our city's insane housing shortage forces you to overpay for a tiny apartment, and then you're forced to share it with a selfish slob. If it's any consolation, millions of other New Yorkers are dealing with similar problems, and though your situation sounds unpleasant, it can be improved through the application of a little native New York roommate wisdom.

First, to cheer you up a bit: Roommates have a lot going for them when compared to living alone. They split the rent, which makes it less of a crushing burden, they help you avoid some of the loneliness people report when they first move to New York, and, most importantly, they force you to deal with someone else, adapt to their issues, and become a more thoughtful person. Sharing your apartment is also much better for the environment: Two people living together produce less waste than two people living apart, and they consume less electricity. So it's not just good for you, it's good for the planet!

Also, as you've probably already figured out, you most likely don't have a choice. A typical guideline for the maximum rent you can afford is 30 percent of your salary. So, if you make $30,000, a typical entry-level wage in NYC, that's $830 per month. It would be impossible to find an apartment by yourself for that amount outside unusual circumstances, like winning an affordable housing lottery or having a relative willing to rent to you at a discount. Even if you made twice that, it might be hard to find a studio or one-bedroom apartment in a neighborhood you want to live in. With a roommate, especially one willing to split a one-bedroom with one of you sleeping in the living room, your options expand dramatically.

This is true no matter what age you are. Unlike in other cities with cheaper rent, it's common in New York for people to live with roommates well into their thirties, and even have roommates after they've paired up in couples. The cost savings is that compelling, and some people genuinely enjoy the companionship of living with others. Even our city's seniors often find it preferable to find a roommate rather than live alone for the same reason as twenty-somethings: It's more affordable and less depressing to live with a roommate than by yourself.

Now, of course, living with one or more people in a small apartment can create conflicts of the sort you've already experienced. The number one piece of advice for avoiding this sort of headache is this: Don't be passive-aggressive. Be aggressive-aggressive. When something annoys you—the half-eaten bowl of Kashi Honey Puffs left to calcify in the sink every single goddamn morning, a mysterious showering method that routinely deposits a quarter inch of fetid water on the bathroom floor, a tolerance for filth that would shock even the most hardened health department inspectors—don't just bottle it up and complain to advice columnists.

No, you need to march right up to the person who has caused you this upset and lay it all on the line. Explain that relationships rest on an essential reciprocity, and while you appreciate them as a person and enjoy their company, you believe they have violated this basic fairness and demand that they change. If you're too nice or shy to do this, a letter slipped under the bedroom door will produce the same effect. You will likely find they have their own share of complaints—maybe they don't like your uptight dependence on shower curtains, or the way you coldly address their girlfriend, or your overall judgmental attitude. This is fine! It's good to get it all out in the open and clear the air.

Once you've established all the issues troubling your tenancy, you should write them down and discuss equitable solutions in an open and forthright manner. For instance, you could agree that dishes in the sink will be washed, but compromise that they need only to be washed once a day, before leaving for work or before going to bed. Or you could agree to clean the bathroom in exchange for your roommate cleaning the fridge. The most contentious issue sounds like visitor privileges, which is very common. The easiest solution is to agree on a set number of nights per week each room-mate may have guests. If they want to hang out more than that, no problem: They can go out to a movie or "Netflix and chill" at the girlfriend's place.

The tenets of this understanding should be documented in a "room-mate contract," which outlines each person's responsibilities, along with the financial details (who pays what for rent, utilities, food, and anything else each month). Each roommate should sign this contract, it should be kept somewhere safe, and it should be referred to or amended as new issues arise. Ideally, this whole process should be initiated *before* you move in together; it's a lot easier to handle new problems once you have a framework in place to deal with them.

I learned this the hard way. My first apartment after college was with Mike, a cousin of my best friend from Park Slope. We had a lot of common interests—graffiti, exploring Chinatown and the Lower East Side, the burgeoning internet scene—but, it quickly turned out, very different approaches to apartment life. He could be messy: I recall, with a shudder, his "linguine *vongole*" dishes left in the sink for days. And he could be loud: He was a DJ on the side and enjoyed spinning records late into the night, a time when many non-DJ people, me included, have a tendency to desire sleep. He was also a notorious skinflint; I remember him leaving me a receipt for two dollars' worth of toilet paper he had bought and complaining when it wasn't immediately paid.

Not that I was perfect, either. I had just come out of a bad breakup, felt pretty lost professionally, and spent a good part of the first few months holed up in my tiny five-by-twelve-foot room feeling anxious and depressed. Even after I cheered up, found a new girlfriend, and started spending most of my time at her place, it seemed like every little thing he did was intended to get on my nerves. Increasingly, I also felt like he was cheating me on the rent—I was paying $1,000 and he was paying $900—even though his room was about 30 percent bigger than mine.

Things devolved badly. After a little more than a year, I wigged out, scribbled a note with the exact dimensions of each of our rooms, and demanded a rent renegotiation. He responded by telling me he'd bought an apartment on First Avenue with all the money he'd saved up, and I had three days to vacate the place. Afterward, even though it turned out for the best (he loved his new apartment and soon thereafter became an internet millionaire, and I ended up hastily moving into my future wife's apartment on Thompson Street), we didn't speak for almost five years.

That unpleasantness could have all been avoided if we'd just set out our rules for cohabitating in a roommate contract at the very beginning, and if we had approached each of our conflicts in the spirit of compromise instead of the spirit of winning. After all, we were friends, and it was obvious that neither of us was perfect. Instead, we let every idiotic disagreement escalate on top of the bad blood left over from the last one until we reached the point where we couldn't stand to look at each other. If I could go back and give my twenty-three-year-old self some advice, I'd say, "Chill out, bro; in a city as dense and tense as New York, you can't afford to have an unhappy home life over stupid shit like this. Try to at least *pretend* to be the mature adult in the room."

I'm confident that you can do a lot better than I did. If you can find it in yourself to communicate openly and honestly with your roommate and cut them a break every once in awhile, I think you'll be surprised at how quickly their behavior will improve, and how much better you'll feel about both them and yourself.

Peace,
Jake

N.B.: Here are six other roommate tips that will help you avoid terrible living situations.

1. Make sure everyone is on the lease, because the worst fights happen when one or more roommates aren't, and then bail, and leave the rest on the hook for the rent.

2. Consider smaller apartments if you can, because it's a hell of a lot easier to get along with just one roommate than it is to deal with a rotating circus of five or six clowns constantly moving in and out.

3. If you ever have to move in with a stranger, ALWAYS check their references, both professional and personal. In this age of Facebook, it takes about ten minutes, and it can save you months of heartache in the unlikely case that they are a psychopath.

4. Never be unfair with a roommate in matters of money—it will come back to haunt you. This is especially true when unevenly splitting rents. In a rent-stabilized apartment, the most you can charge a roommate is 50 percent of the rent; otherwise, they can sue you for an overcharge. Even if you're not rent stabilized, overcharging a roommate usually leads to them getting revenge by making your life a living hell through myriad small but maddening acts of inconsiderate behavior.

5. If possible, try to find apartments in older buildings with thicker walls, which will deaden sound. Even better, find one with rooms on either end of a hallway to give each person more private space.

6. Always get renter's insurance: It could be a lifesaver on those rare occasions where one of your roommates leaves the front door open and all your computers are stolen. Plus, it is usually very affordable, like ten bucks a month or less.

Dear Jake,

I love my new apartment. It's a small studio with good light in the East Village and it's within my price range. Only one problem: The neighbors all appear to be jerks! Now, I admit that some of this might be because I'm new and it seems like they've lived in the building forever. But still, most of them ignore me, and just last week as I was coming in, someone literally let the door slam in my face instead of holding it! Who does that?

Also, my upstairs neighbor has been making a lot of noise late at night. It sounds like banging pots or dragging stuff (bodies?) around. He's an older guy, and I'm kind of scared to go up there and tell him to please knock it off.

Do you have any advice about how to deal with these people?

Sincerely,
East Village Newbie

Dear EVN,

A little neighbor nonsense seems like a relatively small price to pay for a cheap East Village apartment these days, so cheer up—you're already doing better than most of your peers. And, unlike other housing problems like bedbugs, slumlords who let the building go to hell, or intolerable smells from a restaurant downstairs, this one has a simple fix.

For the next month, every time you pass someone in the stairs, vestibule, or hallway of the building, I want you to say, "Hello!" in a bright, loud voice. If they stop, you should add a second comment—something innocuous like "It's so hot today!" or "Happy Friday!" Half of the people will ignore you at first, but after you do it a few times, even the most hardhearted neighbor will likely begin responding with at least a half-assed "What's up?" or "How are you?"

This is your opportunity to strike. Start with a simple question—something like, "Hey, you know I just moved in; do you know if it's cool to store my bike in the basement?" Or, "Do you know if we have roof access?" People love to give advice, and giving them the opportunity to be helpful is a great way to create warm relations. Ideally, your questions will be real ones you actually have; don't fake it if you don't have to.

After a month of this, most neighbors will consider you one of the family and your problems will be solved. You could, of course, take it even further by offering to help the older people in the building carry up their packages, giving the younger families a hand carrying down their strollers, etc. I've always found that these kinds of casual, friendly, neighbor relations go a long way to making a building a more pleasant place to live, and I can guarantee that you will never have a door slammed in your face again.

Why did that happen, by the way? It wasn't because your neighbors are unfriendly louts. And although you are right to suspect that some of them may be concerned about gentrification in the neighborhood and younger residents like you pricing them out, that's probably not the reason, either. My guess is that they were probably following the native rule that you never, ever, let someone into the building you don't recognize.

This goes for everyone: deliverymen, old ladies, young kids, German Airbnb guests, Girl Scouts selling cookies. To the street-smart, somewhat paranoid New Yorker, any of these could actually be burglars or murderers in disguise, and we don't want to be the one to let them tailgate us into the building and thereby be responsible for any headline-grabbing carnage that may ensue. What's more, by applying this rule to everyone, we ensure that we're not acting unconsciously racist and judging potential threats based on the color of a person's skin or their clothes. No one gets allowed in unless we know them.

(For buildings with intercoms, this obviously also includes those times when someone buzzes your apartment and claims to be UPS or the gas company or the police—you never, ever buzz them in. You may, if you wish, go downstairs and check them out, but the important thing is to maintain the security of your building.)

So, I think we've solved everything except your noise issue. This is by far the most common neighbor complaint in the city. First, ask yourself if the noise is really intolerable. After you first move into an apartment, it takes about a month for your brain to settle down and get used to the new environment. During this period of acclimation, unexpected noises will sound louder than usual, and much more annoying. As New York is a dense city, and our apartment buildings are often built from crappy, noise-passing materials, you must make a certain allowance for sound from your neighbors—music, movie explosions, arguments, people walking around upstairs.

Often, just getting used to the sound will make this problem go away. Try to relax. Meditate, take a warm bath before bed, play some soothing music, and see if the noise still bothers you. If it does, buy a white-noise machine. They are cheap and can drown out an impressive array of sounds—even garbage trucks, airplanes and helicopters, and crying children. If that doesn't work, it's time for a delicate conversation with the neighbor. This will go much, much better if you've completed the steps above and have already established a respectful rapport with him (or her). The first time you speak to a neighbor, it should never be "Hey, can you please quiet the fuck down?"

So let's say you are already on "hello" terms with the neighbor. One night, at a reasonable hour after dinner, go upstairs, knock on the door, and say something along the lines of "Hey, I hate to bother you, but the last few nights I've been awakened by some loud banging coming through my ceiling. I know this is annoying, but is there any way you could try to quiet down, not wear your boots in the apartment, or get an area rug to keep it a little quieter?" In my experience, this almost always works on the first try. Once, when we had an upstairs neighbor who had developed an unusual after-midnight woodworking hobby, he not only stopped doing it, but he actually gave us a bottle of wine and an apology card.

However, your neighbor may turn out to be less thoughtful. Perhaps he is too cheap to buy a rug, loves wearing boots indoors, and has been stomping around for twenty-five years with no problems, and he sees your request as an unfair interference with his rights. You could ask again, nicely, but the odds are that you're not going to get any better results than you did the first time. This is the moment to escalate to your super (or if you live in a fancy building, your doorman.)

To do this, you need to already be on their good side. Just as with the neighbors, it is essential to spend the first months in a new building getting to know the people who work there. Know their names and use them: "Hello, Frank, how's it going?" Ask them about themselves: how long they've been working at the building, what they like and don't like. Tip generously at the end of the year and when they help you out with something, and they'll be on your side when troubles arise. If you don't have money, offer food—you can buy an incredible amount of goodwill with a simple plate of cookies.

If your upstairs neighbor refuses to give you satisfaction on the noise, go to the super and ask if he can do anything about it. Often a simple conversation between him and the offending neighbor will cure the problem. If it doesn't, he can help you escalate to the landlord or management company, which is your last line of defense (some people recommend calling 311 or submitting a complaint on NYC.gov, but in my experience, if personal appeals and requests from the landlord haven't worked, getting the city involved isn't going to do anything helpful).

If you've done everything above, and the noise is still intolerable to you, you can usually break the lease and move. This will require getting a lawyer to write you a letter claiming the landlord has breached their obligations to provide a habitable apartment, but this is fairly inexpensive and you will feel better knowing you're not trapped in an apartment you hate. The next time you rent, consider searching for a top-floor apartment (as noise doesn't travel up as much as it travels down) in a prewar building (which always has thicker walls and higher ceilings), with a bedroom that doesn't face the street.

Good luck!
Jake

Dear Jake,

I'm in a real bind. My best friend Susan lives in an apartment in Bushwick that she has recently confirmed is infested by BEDBUGS. She's, of course, completely freaked out—they don't know how they got them (the landlord says it's the first time he's seen them in the building) and the exterminator who came by says the infestation is bad. They'll have to do some exhausting combination of spraying, steaming, and caulking cracks and holes in the wall, which will take at least a week. Oh, and the exterminator recommended that they seal all their clothes and personal items in bags for at least eighteen months to make sure that no bugs survived—he said that just washing the clothes in boiling water wouldn't necessarily kill all of them.

This is all bad enough, but Susan has asked if she can stay at my place in Crown Heights until the extermination is done. I obviously want to help her, but I am worried she will bring bugs into my apartment and they'll destroy my life, too. Oh, and I have roommates—I haven't even told them what's going on. What should I tell her?

Sincerely,
Bugged Out

Dear BO,

Native New Yorkers are brave, but there are some things that scare even us—losing our rent-stabilized lease, slipping in a garbage-juice puddle in August, and of course, the worst calamity of all: bedbugs. I've had friends who survived terrible shit—abusive relationships, cancer, divorce—with complete stoicism be reduced to quivering mental collapse by infestations of these voracious, blood-sucking parasites. So you have every right to be concerned. You have witnessed the chaos they've wrought in your friend's life and don't want to experience the same thing.

If she were to come to stay at your place, any luggage that she brought could be a potential vector of infection. The same goes for her clothes: Research says that bedbugs generally prefer not to travel on clothing because it's too close to the skin, which they find too hot to stay on for very long. This, however, is a slim scientific fact to stake your future on. Even if she didn't carry bedbugs in on her clothes, psychologically you'd always be concerned that she had, and that means every mosquito bite and allergic reaction you have for the next year is going to cause an episode of bedbug psychosis.

These psychological effects are not to be dismissed: My friends who have dealt with bedbugs have compared the aftermath to PTSD, with months or even years of anxiety and sleeplessness following an infestation. So this is something you want to avoid, and there's a simple way around it: If you want to do right by your friend and give her a place to crash, you're going to need to ask her to bring nothing into your apartment: not her clothes, not a toothbrush—nothing.

Here's the process: Once she has secured her things, she is to leave her apartment with nothing but a set of disposable clothing on her back and meet you in a neutral location—a gym would be best, but a Starbucks bathroom will work in a pinch. There, she will strip, place all of her clothes in a garbage bag, and you will examine her for evidence of any bedbugs riding along on her skin or hair. If you think this approach is already too extreme, I will safely assume you have never known anyone who has been cursed with bedbugs.

Familiarize yourself in advance with what the bugs look like. There are plenty of internet guides that will help you distinguish the real thing from similar but non-threatening insects, like beetles and ticks. (But don't spend *too* much time doing this, because it will increase your paranoia later on.) If a shower is available, make her use it, and once you're convinced she's clean, give her some new clothes that you've brought and proceed to your apartment. There, you will need to provide both material support (new toiletries and clothes) and emotional succor (she will be in a vulnerable state for quite awhile).

Will your friend be cool with going through this humiliating ordeal? I suppose it depends on how badly she wants to stay with you, but if you are her only chance at staying in the city and getting to work during the bedbug treatment, she'll probably do whatever you require. Look at the bright side: Your bond will be so much deeper once you've survived this together! True friendship is friendship that has been tested by harrowing ordeals and survived.

Your roommates present an unfortunate complexity. If you tell them the truth, they may be so freaked out that, despite your promise to follow the process above, they still might not let her stay. But if you lie to them and they find out from common friends, or because your bedbug refugee is screaming "bedbugs!" in her sleep or something, it could ruin the mutual trust that good roommate relationships are built on. Sometimes in life you have to make decisions between two imperfect situations—in this case, judge how rational and calm your roommates are and then make the best choice you can.

I will also take this opportunity to mention that my friends who have successfully battled bedbugs say their exterminators strongly advised them to remain in the apartment during the treatment process. The reason is grisly but simple: After spraying the bedbug-killing poison all over the bedroom floor, it is helpful to offer some sort of bait to draw the bastards out of their hiding places in the walls or wherever they're lurking. The bait, in this scenario, is Susan's delicious blood. As the bedbugs traipse toward her in the dead of night following the exterminator's visit, they will be walking right through a poisonous trap. You could reasonably argue that the best place for Susan to stay is not your apartment, but rather right in the heart of darkness itself until the battle is won.

If reading this letter has raised your level of anxiety to an uncomfortable degree, be comforted by a few facts. First, bedbug complaints have been going down in NYC for the last several years. The New York City Department of Housing Preservation and Development (HPD) reported 13,138 complaints in 2011 and only 9,508 in 2015. This is because landlords have gotten better at dealing with infestations (for instance, by inspecting adjacent apartments and having the exterminators visit sites of past infection every three months for follow up), and because New Yorkers have gotten so paranoid about bedbugs that we no longer practice many of the dangerous habits that enable them to spread—taking furniture off the streets, or having one-night stands with people without first inquiring if their apartments are clean (okay, that might actually be going too far).

Second, New York has some of the most progressive laws anywhere when it comes to bedbugs. Since 2010, landlords have been required to give new residential tenants a one-year bedbug-infestation history of both the apartment and the entire building. You should also check for information on adjoining buildings, because bedbugs can find their ways through walls. If the building next door has a lot of complaints, think twice about renting the place. This disclosure, of course, should be taken with a grain of salt, as some landlords aren't the most honest characters, so you should always google any prospective apartment for bedbug complaints and also check the HPD website for a history of bedbug violations.

If all of this fails, and you do rent an infested apartment, or find an infestation visited upon you, your landlord is responsible for paying for the extermination. If they drag their feet on this, pay for it yourself (there are many well-reviewed bedbug exterminators listed on Yelp) and deduct the amount from your rent check. You will probably have to threaten to go to a lawyer (or better yet, go public with a complaint on one of the bedbug registry websites), but they will come around.

Third, and finally, know that there are some upsides to a bedbug infestation. They're a powerful incentive to embrace minimalism, which is a virtue in our materialistic society. Once you put most of your furniture in a dumpster and your clothes in bags for months, you'll come to realize how little of that stuff you needed in the first place, and that knowledge will serve you well for the rest of your life. The bedbug experience will also open your heart to the suffering of anyone who has had their life turned upside down by factors beyond their control.

Sure, this spiritual deepening may be small consolation while you're still in the throes of an episode—scratching, crying, never sleeping, scratching some more—but long term, you will appreciate it and it will make you a warmer, wiser person.

In sympathy,
Jake

N.B.: I practice what I preach. Once a friend of mine casually told me over lunch that his apartment had just been infested; he said it like it was no big deal. I noted that our coats were lying on top of each other on a chair nearby. Long story short, when I got back to my apartment, I stripped naked outside the door, clothes, coat, and all, went inside, changed, and came back and bagged everything right into the trash. The bedbug is a resilient, tenacious adversary, and the only way to defeat them is with a ruthless scorched-Earth approach to the battlefield that is your apartment.

Dear Jake,

I moved to Bed-Stuy a year ago, and I love it—it's a beautiful neighborhood with old brownstones, a great mix of young people and old timers, and my apartment is only eight blocks from the C train. Some new restaurants and coffee shops have opened recently on the avenues, and some weekends I don't even leave the neighborhood because everything I need is here. So, on Monday when I was walking to the train, I saw a big GENTRIFIERS GO HOME! tag painted across one of the stores' roll-down gates. I felt really bad and angry, because even though I'm young and white and probably have a little more money than the people who have lived here a long time, and could therefore be considered a gentrifier, I feel like this IS my home. Am I not improving things by being a good neighbor and spending my money locally? Don't I have a right to live here too?

Sincerely,
Good Gentrifier

————————————

Dear GG,

You certainly have a right to live anywhere in the city you want, and you do seem to genuinely love your new community and want to understand and contribute to it. That's a good attitude, because not all new arrivals are as thoughtful as you are—some don't think about the feelings of the longtime residents at all, and some actively dislike anything old and ungentrified: the dusty bodegas, the raucous stoop parties, the run-down buildings that haven't yet been flipped.

Understanding gentrification takes more than a good attitude, however. First, try to stand in the shoes of the kid who wrote that graffiti and ask yourself why he wants people like you to get out. I'd wager the source of his anger is actually fear: The fear afflicting all natives: that after suffering and surviving through the bad old days, a wave of new, rich arrivals will swamp the neighborhood, drive up the rents, and force them, their family, and all of their friends to disperse further out in Brooklyn, or maybe out of the city all together. Imagine how you'd feel in that situation—powerless and upset and eager to send an unambiguous message to the newcomers.

You might be thinking, "But haven't I, and all the other gentrifiers, brought money and new amenities to a neighborhood that had been deteriorating, neglected by the city government for years?" Yes, you have; you've also probably made the neighborhood safer, because wealthier people are better at getting the attention of politicians and the NYPD; they're also better at getting resources like more foot patrols assigned. These are all good things, except that the locals don't feel like any of it is "for them"—they feel like those new shops and eateries are too expensive to patronize, and they may even feel unwelcome inside because of how they look or how they're dressed. And while they might appreciate a safer neighborhood, they also might feel that when a white person is a victim, the police react like it's a major emergency, but when it's a black or Hispanic person, not so much.

So, to the old timers, you have an anxious situation being overshadowed by a very specific, urgent threat: rising rents. Two-thirds of New Yorkers rent their apartments, and, while half of all renters are protected by some kind of rent stabilization or rent control, everyone here knows what happens when a neighborhood starts to undergo gentrification: The landlords jack up the rent on everyone who isn't stabilized and force them out immediately, and then they use intimidation (constant construction or no repairs at all, physical threats, spurious legal action, etc.) to get rid of everyone else. If it's a really hot market, they might even offer cash buyouts to get the last tenants to leave—but by that point the money is usually not enough to relocate anywhere nearby.

Rents aren't the only costs that go up. As bodegas close and get replaced by higher-end supermarkets, the price of food increases, too. Even at the stores that remain, prices may increase as storekeepers recognize they now have a population of residents who can pay more, or they see their own commercial rent jacked up by their landlords and have to raise prices to compensate. This can also affect neighborhood institutions—the old social clubs, bars, storefront churches, and so on—that may find their rents raised so much that they also have to relocate or close.

(An interesting complication is that there is a small group of longtime residents who might actually welcome your arrival: older homeowners. If you bought your Bed-Stuy brownstone for $15,000 in 1960, and are ready to retire, you can sell it now for a million or two. Of course, that will require you to move, which you may not want to do, especially if you have children or grandchildren living in the house with you. If you want to stay, then you're basically in the same boat as the renters: You have paper wealth that you can't tap, and you have the unhappy experience of seeing prices rise and friends and relatives displaced.)

Now, you, of course, bear very little responsibility for any of this. You're just one person, and you moved to the neighborhood for the same reason everyone else did, because it was affordable to you. In fact, you may have been pushed out of a different neighborhood—say Williamsburg, or the East Village—by the exact same forces that are now impacting your Bed-Stuy neighbors. This is what powers the gentrification cycle: regular people looking for more affordable housing. Usually artists lead the way, because they have the least money and need space to do their work, but they're soon followed by young people on similarly tight budgets, and soon after that, the floodgates open as developers see dollar signs and start aggressively marketing the neighborhood. Sometimes the developers even catalyze this process by recruiting the initial batch of artists and offering them cheap rent (for a time).

The only way to end this cycle of gentrification is to build affordable housing in every neighborhood, and so far, the city and state politicians have not shown a willingness to do that. This is because their biggest donors are the very same real-estate developers who benefit most from gentrification. In the absence of such a building program, gentrification will continue to proceed along the subway lines until it reaches the far edges of the city. The next neighborhood over from Bed-Stuy is already being prepared: East New York. And if Brooklyn is ever totally tapped out, there are parts of Queens and the Bronx that can still be converted.

Do the locals have a right to take their gentrification anger out on you? No, because there is no one in the city who can say they, or their ancestors, have not participated in this process. Take my family: They arrived with the wave of Jews fleeing Russian pogroms around 1900, and after a decade or two in the ghettos of the Lower East Side, they moved uptown and into the Bronx. Their arrival displaced poorer, older waves of immigrants, just as my parents and their friends, two generations later, displaced the working-class Irish and black people who occupied Park Slope in the 1960s and early 1970s. I probably contributed to the gentrification of Chinatown and the South Village by renting apartments there when the areas were still largely inhabited by poorer Chinese and Italian enclaves.

Even if your ancestors go all the way back to the first Dutch settlers, you're part of this gentrification cycle. Think of the local Lenape Indians who were forced out of their historical hunting grounds by new arrivals looking for a place to live. I find this historical perspective consoling; it means that no one can honestly point a finger and say, "This all started when you arrived here!" Not even the residents of Bed-Stuy, who arrived in the 1930s replacing the Jews and Italians who had previously lived there, and who were beginning to move to the newly created suburbs.

If gentrification is unstoppable, and we are all participants in it in some way, what is to be done? For new arrivals, like you, a good first step would be trying to get to know your neighbors—all of your neighbors. Smile and say hello to everyone on the block as often as you can. Try to patronize all of the old stores; that cold hard cash you bring to the neighborhood shouldn't all go to overpriced coffee shops. Finally, band together politically with neighbors when you share common concerns. This could be speaking up for better policing at the community board meeting or coming together with the rent-stabilized tenants in your building to oppose landlord harassment. You'll still be a gentrifier, but you'll be the most positive, thoughtful gentrifier you can be.

We natives should try to do likewise. Instead of directing our fury at the new youngsters in the neighborhood, we should turn it on the true causes of our misery: the developers and the politicians they control. Demanding more affordable housing and voting for local officials who promise to require developers to include it in all new buildings is a much more effective response than spray painting anti-gentrification graffiti on roll-down gates.

This is a lot to ask, I know, from both sides, but if we want to have livable, diverse neighborhoods, we've got to do it. Remember: Today's gentrifiers will be tomorrow's gentrified, so you might as well get the process of understanding and reconciliation started now.

Peace,
Jake

CHAPTER 4

How to Get Around Like a Native New Yorker

Questions

Crowds of men and women attired in the usual costumes! how curious you are to me!

On the ferry-boats, the hundreds and hundreds that cross, returning home, are more curious to me than you suppose;

And you that shall cross from shore to shore years hence, are more to me, and more in my meditations, than you might suppose.

—WALT WHITMAN, "CROSSING BROOKLYN FERRY" FROM *LEAVES OF GRASS*

Dear Jake,

The other day I was coming home from a long, exhausting day at work (I'm a teacher) and I managed to grab a seat on the train, which is pretty rare because my job is on the West Side and all the Midtown office workers usually crowd on before my stop. As the train got to Jay Street, still seven stops from my apartment, a big crowd pushed on. A mother and her kid ended up right in front of me, and the mother looked at me and said, "Could he have your seat?" The kid was at least ten years old.

Now, I work with kids all day and love them, but inwardly I'm screaming, "Are you kidding me? He's not a toddler! I need this seat a lot more than he does!" Instead, I just meekly smiled and got up and fumed about it all the way back home. Was I obligated to give up my seat?

Sincerely,
Tired of Standing

Dear TOS,

I'm constantly amazed by the letters I get about the New York City subway; it's like they crystallize the entire city in microcosm, and any conflict you could face aboveground is duplicated beneath in miniature: brutal competition for precious real estate, merciless clashes between young and old, men and women, rich and poor. To understand the subway—its rules and unspoken etiquette—is to understand New York. No person, however long they have lived here, can be considered a real New Yorker if they only get around by car.

Take your situation: a classic "who deserves this seat more" question. I've received dozens of these inquiries over my years as a columnist. Some are easy: Obviously, you get up for a very old person, or a visibly pregnant woman, or someone who is disabled. But what about other groups: children, the sturdy-looking middle aged, or a woman who *might* be pregnant, but also might just be wearing a puffy coat? How do you decide whether to get up or not?

First, you need to ask yourself how much you really need the seat. Are you so exhausted that getting up is physically painful? Or are you just the regular kind of tired that all New Yorkers feel after a long day of work? Safety first, obviously. We don't want you getting up to give your seat to a kid and then fainting right on top of him. However, it sounds like you were physically able to stand—annoyed, but upright—through the rest of your ride.

Keep in mind that it is very difficult to ask someone to give up their seat. Psychologists have actually studied this and found that asking strangers for a favor is incredibly unpleasant. This is particularly true on a New York subway, where we've been taught to avoid eye contact with other riders and mind our own business. When that mom asked you for your seat, she was doing something difficult, and maybe for a good reason. Some disabilities aren't visible—it's possible that the kid really did need the seat and you were doing a really nice and helpful thing by giving it up.

In fact, I want you to really meditate on that. There are so few times each year when we really get a chance to help a stranger, and thereby make ourselves feel good and earn karmic credits from the city. I've found the subway can be a real opportunity for these kinds of interactions—pointing tourists toward the right train, holding the door for someone sprinting desperately to get on board, or contorting yourself a little so another rider can grab the pole in a crowded car. Helping in these moments makes me feel better about myself, and I look forward to them. For that reason, even when I'm feeling worn out, I try to keep my eyes open for people who need a seat and be the first one up when I spot them.

Now, I'm a man in reasonably good health, and I'm pretty much the least deserving of a seat if there's anyone else on the train who needs to sit down. Even so, I'll take a load off and zone out with my music if there's a seat available—I'm not trying to be a hero at all times. I figure there are enough people who share my general philosophy on subway seat ethics that periodically looking up to confirm I'm still seat-worthy is sufficient. You don't have to be obsessive about it, and most of the time, I get through a whole ride without having to stand. On many occasions, I've even offered my seat to someone—an older woman who looked tired, a teenager carrying a big instrument case, or even a pregnant woman— only to be politely declined. Maybe they were only going one more stop or sitting was uncomfortable for them; you never know.

Of course, riding the subway presents many more conflicts than simply deciding when to give up your seat. I'd like to run through some of the situations people have asked me about; the following is essentially a mini guide to avoiding conflict, producing positivity, and generally being a mensch when taking the train. Here are the basics:

1. When you have the good fortune to score a seat, make sure you take up only one unless this is physically impossible for you— overweight riders have the same right to sit as anyone else, and subway designers seem to have designed the seats for fairly narrow asses. If yours doesn't quite fit, that's not your fault, and nobody has a right to complain about it. For everybody else, don't "manspread" beyond a reasonable allotment of space. What's reasonable? If your legs are touching theirs, it means you need to tighten up that spread. Obviously, any baggage must be placed between your legs, on your lap, or under the seat—taking up a seat for your gym bag is a surefire way to get scolded by justly annoyed commuters.

2. When you can't find a seat and must grab the pole, do not "pole hog" by leaning against it with your body. I'm often sent pictures of people doing this in the most loathsome way, like wrapping themselves around it with both arms and legs, or leaning back against the pole so aggressively that the pole actually creeps into their butt crack. (I actually shuddered when I wrote that last line, but it's real!) The correct way to hold a pole is at chest height, at a distance of twelve inches, to give others room to grab it.

3. Whether standing or sitting, be mindful of those around you, and don't do stuff you would not want done around you. That includes playing

games or listening to music loud enough for others to hear, trimming your nails (a surprisingly frequent occurrence!), conversing loudly to friends, or littering. Eating is another touchy subject. Yes, sometimes life in New York is so fast-paced that the only goddamn time you have to eat your lousy bagel is during your commute, and no one is going to fault you for it. But the rule is "If you can't eat it with one hand, don't eat it at all." I have borne witness to people eating tikka masala on the F train, and it's grotesque—not just due to the risk of spillage, but also the pungent fumes that fill the entire car. Don't be that guy.

4. Do not block the doors. This is as close to a religious commandment as we have in New York, and it's one that's not always easy to follow. Sure, on an empty train you can always find a spot away from the door, but at rush hour you may be the last person to crowd on, and then what do you do? Simple: You must "step off to let the people out," as the conductors say. This means actually stepping onto the platform and waiting slightly to the side to let people move off the train. You are entitled to stand right next to the door, even if it means nudging riders who are about to get on, to keep your spot. What if the train is kind of crowded, you are going only one more stop, and you want to stay by the door to avoid making it difficult to get off? Tough call—if you can flatten yourself in the tiny space between the seats and doors, and thereby avoid blocking people squeezing on (and are willing to accept their unhappy glares), go for it. (This is easier on the new subway cars with more space next to the doors.) But if not, you must move farther inside the car, and simply resign yourself to fighting your way out a few minutes later. Life's tough.

5. Do not use the subway as a moving van. I'm not talking about backpacks and bags; you must take them off, but if they can fit comfortably between your legs or on your lap, you aren't taking up any extra space. I'm not even talking about the tourists coming from JFK—New York is a welcoming place that depends on its tourist industry and we shouldn't begrudge them one rolling suitcase as they head to their hotel. No, here I'm speaking of people transporting furniture,

motorbikes, hundreds of balloons, their Aunt Hazel's coffin, etc. Maybe this kind of stuff is allowable after midnight, when there's plenty of room on the train, but doing it during the day will get you in trouble—if the cops don't hassle you, one of your annoyed fellow passengers will, and the picture they take on their phone will make you an unwilling viral star on the New York City blogs the next day.

6. Finally, once you are off the train, show the same thoughtfulness when standing on the platform, walking up stairs, and riding the escalator that you did while you were inside the train itself. Don't crowd the edge of the platform—it's dangerous and makes it hard for people to get off incoming trains. Always walk to the right on the stairs and stand to the right on the escalators to allow faster-moving people to hasten along to your left. And always, if you are physically able, offer to help parents struggling to carry a stroller. That's a real mitzvah.

The basic idea, through all of these points, is that we've got to crowd more than five million people every weekday on the subway, and if we're going to do that without major bloodshed, we've all got to make an effort to be the most kind, considerate subway riders we can be. While we're doing this, we can think about how blessed we are to have this amazing subway system—one that history has bequeathed to us, which, despite its flaws, is still a fast and efficient way to get around the city and which is one of the great places to see the incredible diversity of New Yorkers up close.

Treasure it!
Jake

N.B.: Many of the things people hate about the subway—the overcrowding at rush hour, the dirty stations, the maddening delays—are due to a state government that underfunds the system by directing an unfair amount of resources to road and infrastructure building upstate. All New Yorkers should vote for politicians, especially on the state level, who make mass transit funding a priority.

Top Ten Forms of NYC Transportation and When to Use Them

1 **YOUR LEGS.** Use 'em if you've got 'em! They'll get you just about anywhere under a mile more conveniently than any other form of conveyance, and here's the good news: They're free to use.

2 **BIKES.** When you need to be somewhere fast, nothing beats a bike, and you get exercise without having to pay for a gym.

3 **SUBWAY.** The default to get you to and from work and between neighborhoods twenty-four hours a day, seven days a week. Any New Yorker who isn't on the subway frequently is doing the city wrong.

4 **BUSES.** They're not typically the fastest, but if you're not in a hurry or need to get home after a day of drinking on the beach at Fort Tilden in the Rockaways, the bus can be a pleasant, scenic conveyance.

5 **FERRIES.** A surprisingly fast way to zip between boroughs if you're near one of the rivers, and, of course, the only way most New Yorkers get to that distant, mysterious place called Staten Island.

6 **CABS.** Even in the age of Uber, hailing a cab on the street is an important skill to have, like when it suddenly starts to rain, or when you don't want your every movement recorded by the internet.

7 **RIDE-HAILING APPS.** Apps like Uber and Lyft are perfect for trips to and from the airport and when you're out drinking late anywhere outside Manhattan and need to get home to pass out; also good for trips to far-off destinations, like Fairway or Ikea.

8 **ELECTRIC SKATEBOARDS.** I'm seeing more of these around New York, and a buddy who commutes from Long Island says it's the best way to get from Penn Station to his office downtown—but he isn't easily embarrassed.

9 **SURREY.** When you're out on Governors Island, rent one of these four-seat surreys with your friends and pedal around enjoying spectacular views of the city skyline.

10 **PEDICABS.** Never used by New Yorkers, they exist purely to sucker tourists into paying $200 for a ride around Central Park.

Dear Jake,

Do you wash your hands after going on the train? I was just walking out of the subway station by work and eating a muffin and I ran into one of my coworkers who rolled her eyes and said, "This is why you're always getting sick! You need to wash your hands before you eat anything." So I told her to stop being such an oppressive germaphobe, but then I started worrying that maybe she is right. What do you natives do?

Sincerely,
Muffin Man on the M Train

Dear MMOTMT,

We natives don't need to wash our hands after using the subway, because we never allow our hands to touch anything during our trip. Seriously—look around the car and notice all the people leaning against the doors or hooking an elbow around the pole. Those are the natives who will not be getting sick while you are suffering through your fourth cold of the winter.

We are also protected by immunity that you do not have. A kid growing up here has to get about thirty vaccinations before he can start public school, and, once there, crowded into ancient buildings with no air circulation, he is going to quickly be exposed to just about every germ. This makes our early years a hellish procession of stuffy noses and throwing up, but by the time we reach adulthood, our immune systems are much hardier than those of transplants such as yourself.

There is a range of resistance, of course, but weaker natives generally leave the city for warmer climates after high school, so the ones who remain tend to be of truly hearty stock. Take me, for instance; I've got two little kids in school now, and these walking germ bombs expose me to more viruses than an emergency room doctor sees, but I get sick maybe once a year.

Of course, there are situations when you can't avoid touching a subway pole, like say if the train comes to a screeching halt and you're thrown up against it; or a subway breakdancer pushes you into one; or you faint, accidentally face-mashing metal on the way down. In those cases, yes, before you touch anything else—food, the doorknob at your office, your face—you must douse those hands in Purell or give them a serious sixty second scrubdown with soap and water. This isn't germophobia; it's common sense.

That's because New York's germs are just like New York's residents: wonderfully diverse, gregarious, and anxious to prove their superiority over new arrivals. One trip on the subway is going to expose you to microscopic life from all over the world. And, just like that Mexican-Korean fusion restaurant you went to last night, the city is going to create germ combinations that have never been seen before, which will be both novel and terrible. You are smart enough not to lick a subway pole—touching a pole and then eating is exactly the same thing.

A few more common-sense native tips to keep you healthy this winter: Avoid rush-hour trains if you can. God could not have designed a more perfect space for germs to travel in, and one strong sneeze can spray half a car. If you must expose yourself to situations like that, compensate by getting plenty of rest; January is a wonderful time to lay off the booze and enjoy some nights inside.

Finally, remember: If you do get sick a lot, that's really a small price to pay for living in the world's greatest city. Even if you lose four weeks to illness, that's still eleven months of good health to enjoy our culture, nightlife, and restaurants. I'd rather be sick as a dog in New York on occasion than fit as a fiddle all year long in Philadelphia.

To healthy living,
Jake

Dear Jake,

I was on the N train yesterday going home from work (I go to the end at Astoria-Ditmars Boulevard). The train was only about a quarter full because it was before rush hour, and around Thirthy-ninth Avenue, I noticed, about ten feet away, this big, tough looking dude with his pants open, stroking his penis and staring at this girl opposite him (I should mention at this point that I'm a five-foot three-inch, thirty-year-old woman). She looked about sixteen and was literally frozen in terror. I didn't know what to do—it felt like this went on for more than a minute, and then suddenly we were at Thirty-sixth Avenue and the girl jumped up and ran off the train, and I ran off after her. She was already down the stairs before I could catch up, and to tell you the truth I felt so guilty about not doing anything that I didn't try to follow her.

The train pulled out of the station. I'm not sure what happened to the guy, but I went down to the station agent at the booth and he said that he could call the police, but by then I was so exhausted by the whole ordeal that I just went back upstairs and took the next train home.

I've been feeling bad about this all week. What could I have done better?

Sincerely,
Perved Out

———————————

Dear PO,

First, don't beat yourself up; you're not the problem here. The problem is men, who are, as a rule, disgusting. Okay, maybe not all men, but have you ever heard of a woman exposing herself on the train to a terrified teenage boy? It just doesn't happen. Or maybe the boys don't report it? Somehow, I doubt it. Every single one of my female friends has had an experience like this on the subway—a gross guy stroking himself, or rubbing up against her, or staring intimidatingly, or saying something nauseating. For many, this has happened repeatedly, starting as early as middle school, and it's damaging. Not only does it make them feel unsafe riding alone, but being repeatedly treated as a sex object can really mess with your self-esteem.

What should you have done? I'm not here to judge you. It sounds like you were frozen in fear, too, and maybe for good reason. Putting yourself in danger does nothing to help the victim. But I think if she hadn't run off the train with you fast behind, you would have summoned up the courage to have intervened. I can tell because your letter shows you to be a concerned, thoughtful person. So, what could you have done?

The native rule book here says that if the perp does not seem dangerous, you should place yourself between him and his victim. This is obviously a very difficult move, but if you're brave, you can stand in front of her and ask quietly if she's all right and would like help. (Do not let the assailant out of your sight while you are doing this—you're dealing with a disturbed individual here, and you must not turn your back on him completely.) Nine times out of ten, she will say yes, and then, as soon as possible, escort her to safety—either off the train at the next stop or to another car. The goal here is to intervene without escalating the situation.

If you don't feel safe enough to intervene with your body, you can use your voice. There are little old ladies on my block who can unleash a blood-curdling banshee roar if a passerby so much as drops a bag of dog poop in their garbage can. If you can summon up that kind of volume (preferably in your toughest New York accent), scream, "What the fuck are you doing?" or "HEY, stop that right now!" The commotion you create should give the victim time to run to safety, and it will certainly attract the attention of the entire subway car, which will be helpful if you need backup.

If you don't feel safe doing that, ask for help from the biggest, friendliest looking bystander you can find. You'll need to look directly into their eyes and say, "Please, can you help me here?" Otherwise, it's quite possible that on a subway car of fifty people, everyone will kind of pretend nothing is going on. This is the famous "bystander effect," in which everyone expects someone else to do something, and so no one does anything. The only way out of it is to ask for specific help from one person. That breaks the spell and then several people will usually rush to your aid.

Once you have helped the victim, there's still more you can do. In recent years, the NYPD has been prosecuting these types of sex crimes more aggressively, so if you're able to take a picture or video of the perp without getting stabbed, please do—you can easily email it to them through the MTA website (anonymously if you prefer). These perverts are usually repeat offenders and many are already known to the police, and even if they can't track them down, they'll at least have the picture for future reference. You'll improve their chances of collaring the guy if you tell the conductor (in the middle of the train) once you're out of danger, and he or she can radio ahead to summon police at the next station.

Subway perverts aren't the only danger on the train. There are still some pickpockets (though this profession has dwindled over the years, as people carry less cash and more credit cards), and frequent "phone snatching," where someone grabs your phone out of your hands just as the doors are closing and runs with it. Are there any tips you can use to keep safe? The MTA helpfully supplies the following:

Use only entrances marked by a green indicator, where there is a clerk present twenty-four hours a day; have your money or MetroCard available; use designated waiting areas [and] ride in the conductor's car during off-peak hours; sit in the center of the car, away from the door, to avoid a purse or chain snatch; cover jewelry: turn stone rings toward the palm side of your hand; stay awake and aware and exit with the crowd.

To this excellent advice, I'd only add a few modern tips: Don't play your music so loud that you lose awareness of what's going on in the car (or annoy the people around you). Keep your phone in your pocket—unless you need it to read or play games, and then hold on tight, especially as the doors open and close. And remember the oldest New York subway wisdom of all: If a crowded train rolls into the station with one mysteriously empty car, do NOT get on. There is a reason it is empty, and you do not want to find out what it is.

Finally, in these troubling times, remember that we're all in this together. Women are not the only people who get intimidated or harassed on the train. If you see a man in a turban or a woman in a hijab being bothered by some racist knucklehead, you can apply all the same advice above and show them New York City's inclusive spirit of welcome toward people of all religions. The same goes for immigrants, LGBTQIA individuals, or members of any other victimized group. It is up to each of us to see that everyone has (in the words of the subway announcer) a "safe and pleasant ride." Do your best to make that happen.

Strength,
Jake

Dear Jake,

I just rented a new apartment in Sunnyside. As soon as I moved in, I noticed there was a bike lane on the street, and I realized that it would be possible to bike over the Fifty-ninth Street Bridge to my job in Midtown. The only problem is that I'm completely terrified by the idea of bicycling in NYC. I know how to ride a bike—that's not the problem—the problem is riding a bike surrounded by New York traffic. Am I being overly neurotic here? How safe is biking? Do you think I can commute every day without getting killed?

Sincerely,
Scared Cyclist

———————————

Dear SC,

A little fear is healthy for a bicyclist in New York. You need to be on high alert to avoid being hit by drivers or running over pedestrians, but too much fear is unnecessary and counterproductive. I've been bicycling all over the city as my primary means of transportation for twenty-five years, and apart from a few close calls with people opening cab doors, I've never had an injury or even a banged-up bike. Once you master a few simple tips, and spend a few dozen hours habituating yourself to the patterns of New York traffic, you'll be fine.

It's worth the effort—biking is the best way to get around most of New York. It's usually quicker than taking the subway and is a source of exercise that doesn't require paying a usurious gym fee. Apart from the costs of your bike, helmet, and the occasional repair, it's completely free. It makes me sad that so many people dismiss the New York bicycling experience as being out of hand because it seems scary. In fact, once you get used to it, it isn't any scarier than walking, and is a lot less scary than taking a cab ride, given how most cabbies drive.

First, some calming statistics: The NYC Department of Transportation estimates that "more than three-quarters of a million New Yorkers ride a bike regularly—250,000 more than just five years ago. It is estimated that over 400,000 cycling trips are made each day in New York City—nearly triple the amount taken fifteen years ago." During this time, severe injuries and fatalities fell from more than "eight per million cycling trips" to a current low of about two per million. That's still too high—it works out to about twenty cyclists killed each year—but balanced against the enormous and growing numbers of riders, it's a very small risk. Much of the increase in safety is due to an extensive network of bike lanes that advocacy groups like Transportation Alternatives have lobbied the city for over the years; the more safety improvements implemented, the more people bike, and the more people bike, the more safety there is in numbers.

That bike lane in front of your house is a great stroke of luck. It means you can probably ride all the way to the bridge *theoretically* separate from motor-vehicle traffic, and once you're on the bridge, you have a great bike lane to get you over into Manhattan. The problem is what to do when you get there: We have great bike lanes on Eighth Avenue, Sixth Avenue, and on Broadway that are protected from traffic by concrete dividers. It's the cross-town streets that are more problematic—as in many areas of the city, in Midtown they're patchwork, and even the streets with bike lanes often have trucks blocking them. See if you can chart out a path that sticks to the bike lanes and consider, until your confidence grows, walking your bike on the sidewalk during the parts of the trip that feel too dicey.

Once you start biking, take it slow; that'll keep you safe and prevent you from getting too sweaty on the way to the office (once you start going faster, you'll want to keep a change of clothes at work or find a gym to shower at). Always obey the law: Pay attention to red lights and stop signs, never bike on the sidewalk (unless you're under twelve, in which case, congratulations on a bold reading choice!), never "salmon" against the flow of traffic, and make sure your bike has a headlight and taillight if you're ever riding at night. Following these laws won't just keep you from getting an expensive ticket (I have plenty of friends who have caught $200 fines for running red lights on their bikes), but they'll protect you from collisions, and they'll help improve the reputation of all bicyclists in New York. We're often judged based on the behavior of a few bad apples—the idiots who bike with no hands the wrong way up a street while blasting music on their headphones and then hit some poor senior citizen.

What about safety tips? My number one piece of advice is never assume you know what anyone else on the road is going to do. In fact, assume everyone is going to make the wrong choice—turn without looking, obliviously step out into the street while talking on a phone, or open a taxi door without checking to see if you're coming. If you always assume the worst, then you'll never be surprised. You can make things even safer by making eye contact with drivers before you pass in front of their vehicles, yield to all pedestrians, no matter how egregiously they're jaywalking, and by not biking distractedly; even though the law allows you to wear one earbud (but not two), keep the music down and focus on the street.

You should also always wear a helmet. Some bike advocates point to statistics that suggest helmets don't make much of a difference—if you get run over by an unlicensed box-truck driver, a piece of styrofoam around your head won't matter—but I know cyclists who have saved themselves a trip to the emergency room after lesser accidents by wearing head protection, and I always wear one on every trip. The way I think about it is, sure, it may not save me, but it might, and if the worst does happen, do I really want my friends and family at my funeral saying, "God, if only he was wearing a helmet?" Wear it for them.

Biking has become a bit of a political hot potato in New York recently; often, neighborhoods that haven't had bike lanes object to their installation because vocal drivers feel they'll slow down traffic or take up parking spaces. Similar fights have been breaking out over new Citi Bike locations. We on the bicyclist side respond that bike lanes actually make the streets safer for everyone (because drivers don't have to worry about cyclists weaving in and out of lanes and pedestrians know where the bicyclists are going to be). This has been proven in studies showing reduced pedestrian and bike fatalities on streets with new bike lanes—without any major reduction in traffic speeds below the legal limit, which the cars should be following anyway. In most parts of NYC, that's twenty-five miles per hour.

If you find yourself cycling a lot, consider going to the community board meetings when transit planning is discussed and speak up—the faster we can get a bike lane on every block in the city, the safer we'll make New York.

To a greener Earth,
Jake

N.B.: Citi Bike is a great option if you want to test the waters before buying a bike. It's currently $169 per year for unlimited forty-five-minute rides, and there are stations all over Manhattan and in many neighborhoods in Brooklyn and Queens, including Sunnyside. It's also great even when you own a bike; I use it for short trips around Manhattan when I've taken the subway in, as well as for rides to or from work when I've left my bike in the wrong place.

Dear Jake,

I recently moved in with my boyfriend in Carroll Gardens. It's a beautiful neighborhood, and even though his apartment is small, it gets a lot of light. There's only one problem: his goddamned car. You see, he's got family upstate, and he drives up to see them once or twice a month in his old Toyota. The rest of the time it mostly sits on the block unused. We talk about taking trips out of the city, but our weekends are pretty busy with friends and chores, and I think we took maybe two trips with it last year. We also don't have much reason to use it in the city; besides weekly trips to the Fairway Market in Red Hook, we've gone to the beach in the Rockaways a few times and once drove to Ikea, but that's it.

Anyway, ever since I moved in, he's been making me do alternate side parking for him. He says because my job's hours are flexible (I'm a writer) and his aren't (he works in tech), it really helps him out if I can do it. But I *hate* this responsibility—it's a two-hour ordeal twice a week, and it's beginning to drive me crazy. Is this fair? What should I do?

Yours truly,
Alternately Annoyed

Dear AA,

That is indeed a tough situation! Obviously, you knew your boyfriend had this car before you moved in, but if you didn't agree in advance that you'd be responsible for moving it back and forth during street cleaning, twice a week, month after goddamned month, well, that seems like a big surprise to spring on someone without a lot of discussion first. Is he offering you anything in return besides his love and affection? For instance, doing more of the housework, or letting you choose what TV shows you guys watch together, or reducing your share of the rent?

If not, consider asking for that quid pro quo. Even though you might be able to get a little work done during the time you're waiting inside the car during alternate-side duties, it's probably hard to concentrate—you've got to get in the car, double park, wait for the street cleaner to pass, and then you have to watch all the other double-parked cars like a hawk to make sure none of them weasel into your spot. Sometimes people actually move early, and then a traffic cop will arrive, and everyone will have to move back and wait until the final minute of the no-parking period expires. It's exhausting just thinking about it!

For this reason, and many others, I've never owned a car in the twenty years I've lived as an adult in New York. Growing up with my parents, I saw what a hassle car ownership was—this was back in the '80s when car break-ins were so common that every vehicle had a "no valuables" sign taped to the window, and at least twice a year on our block, cars were mysteriously lit on fire. Really—arson was a popular teen hobby back then. Then there were the constant repairs necessitated by our harsh New York winters, fender-benders with other terrible urban drivers, the parking tickets, the speeding tickets, and the money my parents had to pay to that one bicyclist they dinged up near Prospect Park. But beyond all of these problems, parking was by far the thing they complained about the most, and the topic that they continue to complain about all these years later. I'd say 50 percent of my parents' waking hours are devoted to thinking about parking—where to park, remembering where they parked, how hard it is to park, etc.

Why is it such a hassle? Simple: Have you ever noticed the price for a garage near your apartment? It's probably something like $400 a month, not including tax. So, parking on the street is actually a very valuable commodity, and if the city prices it at $0, which they do on any street that doesn't have meters, demand is going to be very, very high. Now, as you've discovered, just because you don't pay in dollars doesn't mean you don't pay—instead, you're paying with your time and stress. Maybe it's worth asking your boyfriend if getting you this upset is worth the $400 he could spend on a garage space. Or better yet, whether it'd be worth it to try to give up the car entirely and see what happens.

After all, cars are dangerous, with drivers killing hundreds of people a year in New York City alone, and they're horrible for the environment compared to mass transit. And then there are the ridiculous lengths New Yorkers sometimes go to in order to hold a space. There's an old lady on my block who will sometimes park herself in a chair for two hours in the street outside her house, waiting for her daughter to come home to claim the spot. Just last month I read a story about a drug dealer nearby who'd actually constructed his own "no standing" zone with traffic cones so his clients wouldn't have to double park while they picked up their cocaine (he was caught because people on the block complained—not about the drug dealing, but about hogging the parking). And in winter, forget about it: Some people afflicted with Car-Owner Derangement Syndrome believe that if they shovel out their car, the space belongs to them until the snow melts, and they will go absolutely bonkers if someone else parks there—slashing tires, breaking windows, etc.

Do you really want to become one of these anti-zen people? Sure, there are some situations where owning a car is a requirement, even in New York. People who live or work in "transit deserts" (more than ten blocks from the subway) and disabled people—no one is going to begrudge them the right to drive. Of course, transit deserts often have ample parking, including driveways, and the elderly and disabled can often take advantage of handicapped-parking zones to avoid some of the hassles of car ownership. People who really need cars in New York often have a lot less hassle owning them than people who don't: That is, people like your boyfriend, who *sort of* needs a car—after all, visiting his family would be a bit more difficult without it—but who could probably make do without one.

So what if you drove your boyfriend's car upstate and left it there for a month? You might discover other adequate ways to get back and forth, like New York's great regional rail lines. Or you could try renting as needed; often companies get special rates, and if you rent small cars and only do it once a month, you might discover that it's cheaper compared to the cost of car ownership (factoring in the cost of your aggravation).

It's true that car rental costs in NYC are obscenely overpriced compared to other regions, but there are workarounds—check the rental rates at Newark Airport, or in places a little upstate like Brewster, NY, where certain car rental companies will pick you up from the Metro-North train station for free.

For trips within the city that can't easily be done by subway, there's Uber and its many competitors. Even a trip to Ikea is easy without a car; there are vans waiting on the curb that will transport your stuff for a reasonable fee, as well as an affordable delivery service offered by the store for moving large items. The same goes for other destination stores, like Fairway Market and Whole Foods—delivery is often cheap, and it's much easier than dealing with traffic and finding a parking space when you get back.

About 65 percent of your New York neighbors have done this same calculation and decided that car ownership isn't worth the money and stress. I think you'll find that if you take a vacation from your car, you'll end up feeling the same way, and you'll realize how free you can be without worrying about where you parked or what time you need to move it. Spread this gospel to your other car-owning friends!

Enjoy walking more,
Jake

N.B.: I'm often asked whether car ownership is acceptable for people who own second homes outside New York City. My answer is that if you own a second home you're wealthy enough to afford a garage in the city, and it's wrong, morally, to be using up precious street parking for free when other, poorer people need it more.

Dear Jake,

The other night I flew back to town from Chicago and landed at LaGuardia. The flight was delayed, but when I got in two hours late, I was hoping to at least be able to get home in a normal amount of time. No chance—traffic was at a standstill, the line for taxis wrapped around the terminal, and all the Uber drivers were either booked or couldn't get through the traffic blockade.

Why is New York such a third-world country when it comes to airports? Come to think of it, why is it such a third-world country when it comes to all transportation? Have you ever been to a city like London or Shanghai? They're making us look like rank amateurs with their new subways and maglev trains. Why can't we have that stuff?

Sincerely,
Trapped in Traffic

———————————

Dear TIT,

Let's not get carried away. LaGuardia might be an aging, congested airport with all the charm of a portable toilet that's been tipped over in a frat hazing incident, but have you ever actually been to a third-world airport? I don't think you're going to be calling Uber from outside the terminal in Aleppo, assuming your plane is even able to land without bullets rupturing the fuel tanks. So let's tone down the rhetoric and agree that LaGuardia, like New York's other infrastructure, has "room for improvement."

The reason that some of our airports, bridges, tunnels, subways, and commuter rail lines are in poor shape is because of decades of underfunding by the state and federal government. Many New Yorkers, even natives, don't realize that most of these structures, including the entire subway system, are controlled entirely by the state. As you can imagine, the priorities of our state representatives differ substantially from those of our city elected officials. For years, when decisions were made in Albany, downstate projects were underfunded, and roads and bridges upstate got more money than they deserved. Some of this was because New York City was legitimately doing better than Rochester or Buffalo, and the state thought they could use the construction jobs more than we could, but some of it was just pure politics—the New York State Senate and State Assembly have many powerful members who represent districts outside the city.

Some priorities change as different administrations come and go. Currently, Governor Andrew Cuomo has been directing money toward some downstate projects, including the rehabilitation of LaGuardia, complete with an AirTrain connecting to the 7 subway line (though there's considerable debate over whether this will save any significant commuting time to and from the city). Some of the congestion you experienced may have actually been caused by that construction; they're ripping up the roads all around the airport. The state has also been supportive of some new bridge work, including a replacement for the Kosciuszko Bridge on the Brooklyn-Queens Expressway (BQE), which was beginning to develop potholes so big that you could see the boats on Newtown Creek through the deck when you drove over it.

There have also been at least five huge-capital projects around the subway and rail lines: the completion of the Second Avenue subway up to Ninety-sixth Street, the extension of the 7 line to Hudson Yards, the East Side Access project bringing LIRR trains to Grand Central, and a massive Fulton Street Transit Center down by the newly reconstructed World Trade Center. On top of that, many of the tunnels that were damaged during Hurricane Sandy are being rebuilt with improved signals and amenities, like Wi-Fi, countdown clocks, and renovated stations. It might not be a gleaming new system like they can build in a city in China (where an authoritarian government doesn't have to consult its citizens or perform environmental reviews before breaking ground for a new project), but it shouldn't be dismissed, and when you think about it, it's pretty impressive that projects of this magnitude can get built in one of the most congested, expensive cities in the world. I took a tour of the

Second Avenue subway extension when it was still being built, and I can tell you that it's amazing that they were able to build that enormous tunnel under the street without irrevocably damaging any of the residential buildings or stores above it.

What about the future, assuming we survive President Trump and global warming? I think we have a lot to look forward to in terms of getting around New York. First, private cars are going to be a thing of the past. Self-driving cars are already being tested in Phoenix and Pittsburgh, and in a decade or two they'll be working the streets of New York. Imagine a fleet of fifty thousand of them patrolling the city—available in two minutes through services like Uber and far cheaper than cabs because they require no drivers. Lots of people who need cars today to get to work and back will be able to get rid of them, and over time, most people will realize that sharing a car is far cheaper, more environmentally friendly, and more convenient than owning one yourself and letting it sit unused on the street 97 percent of the time.

Since the self-driving cars won't need to park on city streets (they'll either always be moving or will park at lots in far off places like airports overnight), imagine how much space that'll free up on each block. Instead of two lanes of cars, you could have grass medians, bike lanes, small plazas to sit in, or playgrounds. The whole city is going to start looking like one of those pretty European downtowns. You're going to love it! Picture yourself sitting outside your apartment, enjoying the cleaner air, and thinking back to the days when we actually used our precious urban space for free car parking. It's going to seem insane in retrospect.

A full self-driving fleet will have other benefits: Many parking lots in the city will be made available for replacement by housing, which we desperately need, and taxes can be added to the price of rides to make sure that the new system funds mass transit, instead of underpricing it. That could give us desperately needed money to continue expanding our subway system to places it does not yet reach. There are many subway-expansion proposals that have been floated over the years—the most likely is completing the Second Avenue subway so it gets all the way downtown, but there are others. My favorite is the Triboro line, which would circle the city from the Bronx in Hunts Point, through Astoria and Jackson Heights in Queens, down through East New York in Brooklyn, and finally ending up in Bay Ridge (or Staten Island, if we dug a tunnel!).

The paradise I've described here will not come without some serious downsides. The main one is loss of jobs for taxi and truck drivers, as their work is increasingly automated. With luck, the transition will be slow enough that our elected officials can create retraining programs to avoid hardships for these workers. In particular, the advent of self-driving cars will create massive construction needs as we tear up our street infrastructure and replace it—that will require tens of thousands of construction workers, some of whom can be drawn from the ranks of current drivers. Others could be retrained into new twenty-first-century careers, such as self-driving car maintenance and programming.

Fewer cars would also mean less wear and tear on the roads, and thus less money needed for road repairs. Beyond retraining workers, the cash could be redirected to all sorts of new projects, like a bridge to Governors Island, a dozen new ferry lines, an expansion of our very successful express Select Bus Service, or enhanced protection from climate change—say a giant berm surrounding Manhattan with a bike lane on top. In short, in the relatively near future, New York is going to be a transit paradise. We could even get there faster if our politicians were willing to invest more money in infrastructure. California has been doing a good job with this by raising sales tax for transit projects and authorizing a huge bond issuance, taking advantage of today's very low interest rates, to sponsor hundreds of billions of dollars in transportation improvements.

New York could easily do the same. Consider donating to and voting for pro-transit state representatives or joining one of the transit advocacy organizations if you want that to happen.

To a brighter future,
Jake

CHAPTER 5

How to Deal with Others Like a Native New Yorker

Questions

My favorite thing about New York is the people, because I think they're misunderstood. I don't think people realize how kind New York people are.

—BILL MURRAY

Dear Jake,

I have a problem: Whenever I walk down the street, those people who say, "Do you have a second to support the environment?" target me as the kind of sucker who doesn't know how to just ignore them and keep walking. Yes, I am a bleeding-heart, sign-any-petition kind of guy, but it's begun to annoy me because I just can't seem to say no. This is also a problem with aspiring hip-hop artists who push their CDs into my hands, kids raising money for their basketball teams, and the Orthodox guys who ask, "Are you Jewish?" and then make you put on the head gear and pray with them. Each of these things has happened to me more than once! How do you jaded natives deal with these people?

Sincerely,
Really Late All the Time

Dear RLATT,

How do we deal with street blockers? Simple: We don't deal with them. We pretend they don't exist, and if they physically accost us by standing directly in our path or trying to push something into our hands, well, that CD or clipboard might just get elbowed into the street. It's true! There's nothing quite as satisfying as watching a little old lady shoulder one of these jerks out of the way. That small act of justified aggression is the tip of the spear preventing New York's streets from degenerating into an absolute nightmare of grabby hands, aggressive peddlers, and scam artists.

Your problem is that, like many transplants, you misunderstand what it means to be polite to others. Maybe in Minneapolis it means accommodating any stranger who crosses your path and indulging their requests, no matter how outrageous or annoying, with a smile. But in New York, being polite means *not getting in anyone else's way*. If someone violates this very, very simple rule, you have no obligation to them. In fact, you have an obligation to every other New Yorker to be as unaccommodating as possible to ensure they quickly learn how this city works.

Why must you be so uncompromising here? Let me address each of the situations you mentioned.

1. **Signature predators:** These people, who often work in pairs, are employed in a grifting scheme. They are often young people who have been promised jobs "helping charities," but once they start, they usually discover they are working on commission for an evil business. They don't actually want your signature to save the environment; they want to get your credit card number for a recurring donation, out of which their bosses will keep the vast majority and only pennies will make it to the charity they claim to represent. It is absolutely imperative that you donate directly to the charity of your choice through their website, which will ensure the money goes where it should, and that young people aren't being turned out on the street like hookers by save-the-polar-bear pimps.

2. **Hip-hop artists and mixtape pushers:** This is a fairly straightforward street hustle where a young man (I've never seen a woman) pushes a CD into your hand and then claims you've agreed to buy it. Just drop it and walk on. A variation, where the mixtape pusher actually tries to get you to listen to the tape on a pair of headphones, is rarer, but you still see it in Times Square and on Broadway near Houston sometimes. Simply dodge and walk on—you have no obligation to support their music careers, and in most cases, these guys aren't actually musicians; they're just street entrepreneurs pushing a product they didn't even create.

3. **Basketball grifters:** another classic street hustle. It comes in many variations, from kids selling candy on the street to "pay for their basketball uniforms," to kids with a xeroxed copy of a form saying their coach has asked them to raise money to get them to their championship game out of state. In New York City, school children are not

tasked with raising money in this way—it would create a comically large liability for the school if they were injured or kidnapped while out begging strangers for cash. Instead, school uniforms and trips are funded out of the school budget, or by bake sales and safer fundraising mechanisms. These kids are raising money, but they are raising it for themselves. While you should respect their industriousness, there are more effective ways to give to after-school sports, including donating to the venerable Police Athletic League.

4. **Religious proselytizers:** In New York, the perpetrators are Orthodox Jews, particularly followers of Chabad, also known as the Lubavitch movement—most of the other Jewish sects don't believe in trying to convert anyone, because they believe God has ordained who is Jewish in advance. Sometimes you see Jehovah's Witnesses, Scientologists, or Mormons working a literature stand or going door-to-door, but they are much easier to avoid since they don't try to grab you on the street. The Chabadniks are more aggressive. They often come out before the Jewish holidays and stop any man (they usually don't talk to women because of religious rules) who looks the least bit Jewish, and then they ask whether you're a member of the tribe, and whether you'll pray with them. They do it because they believe they get points with God for each lapsed Jew they bring back into the Orthodox fold, even if it's just for a few minutes of prayer on the street. How should you respond? You could try "Am I Jewish? What business is it of yours?" but I've done this and they just take it as encouragement. Lying, if you are Jewish, is a shameful thing to do—our people didn't suffer for two thousand years so you could deny your Judaism just to avoid getting hassled by some black-hat teenagers. No, the correct thing to do is to smile, wish them a Happy Hanukkah or Rosh Hashanah, and keep on walking, ignoring their increasingly desperate pleas to start a conversation. Do not feel even a twinge of guilt here! Yes, New Yorkers do believe in religious tolerance (which is why so many Orthodox groups have settled here), but we also believe just as fervently in your right to privacy—I've

heard that "none of your fucking business" was actually the original city motto.

Anyway, you see the theme here: When New Yorkers sense that someone is attempting to break the local social contract and abscond with some of our time or money, we just keep moving and assume that all others will do the same—only a tourist or very recent arrival would fall for these tricks. I can only say that while it is very kind to want to help others, you help no one if you are just doing it out of a sense of anxiety, fear, or obligation. True compassion for others involves seeing them for who they really are and acting accordingly, which in this case means seeing them as grifters and going about your business. If it makes you feel better, remember that a simple smile costs you zero time or money—try striding briskly by with a friendly grin and a "Sorry!" if you feel the need for a verbal rejection.

The law in New York says you can't obstruct the flow of traffic on a sidewalk, but this is rarely enforced unless someone is really doing something crazy—lying prostrate or setting up a tent. So the only way we're going to keep traffic flowing is if we all pitch in here. Once these guys realize no one is stopping, the business model will slowly fade and we'll have our streets back for their intended purpose: walking as fast as we can while dodging waddling tourists.

Please do your best to summon up some courage and do your part!

Sincerely,
Jake

Dear Jake,

There's this homeless guy outside the supermarket who I pass every morning on the way to work. I used to give him money a couple of times a week, but after a while I stopped. He usually says, "Have a blessed day!" to everyone who passes, whether they give him money or not, but now whenever I pass, he kind of gives me the side-eye and either says nothing or says, "Have a nice day!" in a nasty way. It's my money, right? Aren't I allowed to decide who to give it to without getting attitude?

Yours truly,
Not Feeling Very Blessed

Dear NFVB,

You are clearly a more generous person than most of the New Yorkers I know, who wouldn't give even one dollar to a guy working the same spot every day. That gentleman is running a small business on the sidewalk in a city with many homeless people who desperately need your financial support; giving to him is a poor use of your charity dollars. So, no, you shouldn't feel bad—although if his sassing is getting to you, perhaps you should consider walking on the other side of the street until he forgets who you are.

New Yorkers, especially native New Yorkers, have a bad rep for being insensitive, for being the kind of people who could step over someone bleeding to death on the street without a thought beyond "this annoying gunshot victim is going to make me late for work." Some of this comes from tourists who observe us on their visits walking right past the homeless without a second look. This, of course, is a misunderstanding—first, if you spend a few minutes observing any homeless person actively raising funds, you'll see plenty of New Yorkers who stop to give a dollar or more, or a half sandwich, a cup of coffee, etc. Second, just because a New

In New York you've got to have all the luck.

—CHARLES BUKOWSKI

Yorker prefers not to donate to someone on the street does not mean they are uncharitable.

Our city has had a homeless crisis since at least the 1970s when, after a series of scandals, the state mental hospitals were largely emptied, and at the same time, single-room occupancy ("fleabag") hotels were closed down. This put a large population of mentally ill, often chemically dependent, people on the streets. According to the Coalition for the Homeless, there were more than sixty thousand homeless people in New York City at the end of 2017. Most of them are in the city's shelter system, and only a relatively small percentage can be seen panhandling on the subways and street corners.

It's important to recognize that the street homeless are a small part of a larger crisis. Starting in the 1980s, as the city began its long recovery from the "bad old days," real estate began to increase in value and rents began to go up. The city, state, and federal governments didn't step up to the plate to build enough affordable housing, and increasing numbers of poor families began to find themselves on the street. In New York City, thankfully, the law requires the city to find everyone emergency housing—although it's often terrible, in crumbling, dangerous shelters; dilapidated apartments rented by slumlords to the city for $3,000 a month each; or else in by-the-hour hot-sheet motels on the outskirts of the city. This population, which comprises the vast majority of the city's homeless, typically does not beg. In fact, many of them work multiple low-wage jobs but still cannot afford basic housing. You might see them riding on the subway late at night with their suitcases; whole families nodding off as they trek from one emergency placement to another.

Your question concerns the smaller group of street homeless. The reason longtime New Yorkers prefer not to give to these people is that they frequently have addictions to alcohol or drugs, and the money you give just enables them to indulge those habits. Better to give to charities, like the Doe Fund, Bowery Mission, or City Harvest, which target the real needs of this population: drug and mental illness counseling, shelter, meals, and jobs. I have a friend who sets their giving based on the number of homeless people he passes every day: He gives one dollar for each of them and donates this sum to City Harvest at the end of the month.

The best way to help is to pick the charities you like and set a recurring donation. Giving like this ensures that your generosity won't go to waste, or be misspent, and that you won't forget to give, or donate only to people with the most compelling signs on the street corners with the highest traffic. Often it's the homeless who *can't* hustle for money who are the most desperate, and your support of good charities ensures they will get the help they need. Of course, you can supplement this with a few dollars here and there—I go with my gut and contradict my own advice from time to time and give to people who strike me as truly needy.

More often, though, I do my giving online only, and I offer only eye contact, a smile, and sometimes a "good morning" or "hello." That's a simple way to acknowledge the homeless person and give him the same respect you'd give to any other New Yorker. I've read that, for some people, the worst part of being homeless is feeling invisible, and this is one easy way to help with that. Plus, it's good for you: Expanding your circle of empathy from yourself and your family and friends to encompass less-fortunate strangers is one of the best ways of reducing self-centered egotism and the suffering it creates.

I want to return to the tens of thousands of people who are homeless right now in our city who you do not see begging on the street because they're too busy trying to find emergency shelter for themselves and their families. Yes, they are helped by people giving to some of the charities named above, but what they need most of all is concerted political action to get better shelters built and to have more affordable housing erected around the city. Giving to advocacy groups, like the Coalition for the Homeless, and supporting politicians who make housing for the poor a top priority is a good way to help this group, which, sadly, is expanding every year as housing prices go up.

Sincerely,
Jake

Top Ten Ways to Be Kind in NYC

1 Giving up your seat on the subway or bus. Do this a few hundred times and you're definitely going to heaven when you die. (Heaven, for a New Yorker, is a rent-controlled apartment near Prospect or Central Park.)

2 Holding the subway station exit door so it doesn't slam in the face of the person behind you—people who slip through without holding it for the next person are selfish and cruel.

3 Saying hello to your neighbors—bonus points if you learn and remember their names.

4 Giving half of your sandwich to your stressed-out coworker who hasn't had time to get lunch. This kindness will be remembered the next time you screw up and need their help.

5 Donating money to the less fortunate through great New York charities, like City Harvest and God's Love We Deliver, or by volunteering with them.

6 Shoveling out your neighbors' sidewalks or cars after it snows—this is especially helpful to the elderly who often can't do it themselves

7 Donating your non-bedbug-infested furniture to Housing Works, one of our city's great charities. They also accept books and clothes.

8 Helping your friends move. There's no greater proof of friendship than carrying a couch up four flights of stairs on a Saturday in August.

9 Placing your garbage correctly in the can. If you're trying to balance your soda bottle on top, that means it's too full.

10 Giving newcomers the benefit of your hard-won urban expertise. You don't have to write a book, but explaining to a new arrival how a MetroCard vending machine works could really help them out.

Dear Jake,

I live on the block from hell, literally. There's a leather bar across the street with a kind of underworld vibe, and after it closes, the patrons stumble out and all sorts of bad behavior ensues, of which peeing against the wall opposite my apartment is the least offensive. There's also plenty of screaming arguments and very public displays of affection. All of this makes it hard to sleep at least three nights a week.

The situation isn't much better during the day! The bar is closed, but there's a street meat stand on the corner, and the smoke wafts pretty much directly into my building, so you can't open the windows without gagging on fiery flesh fumes. And, if it's summer, a fake Mister Softee truck ("Mr. Frostee?") parks nearby to subject me to jingle-based psychological warfare over and over—and it's loud enough to penetrate the closed windows!

I recognize that I should've done more research about the block before getting this apartment, but the rent is a good deal and I don't want to move if I can help it. Is there anything I can do to deal with all this crap and make my local environment a better place to live?

Sincerely,
In Hell

Dear IH,

Wow, I'm genuinely impressed by how unbearable this sounds. I've had friends with all sorts of bad apartment location problems—places in Chinatown that smelled intensely of garbage all summer, or ones so close to the bridge that the windows rattled when the train passed (just like in the movies!), or above restaurants where the smells, vermin, and noise combined into a toxic trifecta of terribleness. But you've got it at least that bad, and probably worse.

This is a good moment to highlight the advice you gave about checking out an apartment before you sign a lease. Yes, in the hyper-competitive world of NYC renting, it can be hard to find the time to conduct a full-scale investigation, but usually you can squeeze in a quick online information-gathering session to check for things like 311 complaints on the block, or Yelp reviews of the local restaurants and bars, which will usually show noise or vermin complaints. If you can, spending fifteen minutes in the apartment with the windows open just listening (and smelling) can teach you a lot. So can sitting on the stoop for twenty minutes on a Friday night. If you fail to do this vital research, then you have no one to blame but yourself.

I'll level with you: These problems will be difficult to solve, and it's often much easier to just find a new apartment than spend months or years fighting to make your current one more habitable. But since you've chosen to stay, I'll give you the best advice I can. Luckily, all of your problems seem to share a common thread: They're caused by people doing infuriating and inconsiderate stuff on the street and can be addressed using a common set of solutions honed by annoyed New Yorkers and passed down from one generation to the next.

First, speak to the proprietors of the bar, outdoor grill, and soft-serve truck, and in a polite, friendly way, express your concerns and make it clear that their behavior is driving you insane. Sometimes this simple step will be enough: The bar could post a few signs telling their patrons to keep it down and refrain from outdoor sex on the block, the grill could position its exhaust port in a different direction or move to a new spot, and "Mr. Frostee" might be willing to switch off the music. Of course, this is very optimistic, and it's quite possible other annoyed residents have already made these requests and been rebuffed or ignored.

So it will probably soon be time to call 311 to report your complaints (or report them online at NYC.gov). The threat of escalating fines has a way of motivating businesspeople in a way that polite complaining does not. It helps to know the law here. Though it is illegal to urinate or copulate in public, this is not the bar owner's problem; the tickets would go to the drunk patrons. It would be better to hit the bar with a noise complaint, which is a strategy that will also work on "Mr. Frostee." The city has strict noise laws, which generally limit sound from 10 P.M. to 7 A.M., and make it illegal to play a jingle when an ice-cream truck is parked. Be very specific with the 311 operator about which law is being violated, and keep a record of the time and substance of each of your complaints—it will help if you need to escalate further.

What does that escalation look like? Let's say the street meat guy has ignored your pleas to move, does not appear to be violating any sanitary laws, and has his vending permits completely in order. To get satisfaction here, you're going to need to organize with your neighbors and convince him that you can make his life so difficult that it's not worth fighting you. I'm guessing your block has no block association, because if it did, this work would already have been done: The association would've politely informed the grill man that they were going to set up a picket line to protest, or they would've called the local precinct every time he illegally blocks traffic to move his grilling rig. These threats are much more effective coming from several dozen members of an association than from one annoyed neighbor.

Once you have an association set up, you can also call in for backup from the local community board, or your city assembly representative, who can help you cut through the red tape, mediate seemingly unsolvable conflicts, or make it clear that failure to comply will result in real consequences—say a complaint to the State Liquor Authority the next time the bar's license is up for renewal. Remember: This is a war of attrition, and your goal is to simply wear down the opposing side until they give in. Make it clear to everyone that's what you intend to do, and that you will stick with it for months or years until these provocations are ended.

Is it right to embark on this crusade? You did move to the block after the bar, ice-cream truck, and meat stand were in place—as a recent arrival, do you have the moral standing to demand all of this change just because you can't deal with the noise and smells? After all, most longtime residents have long since gotten used to it, or else gone deaf from the racket and anosmic from the stench. Maybe some of them even like the block exactly as it is, hellish though it may seem to you. I'd recommend at least talking to a few neighbors, particularly the old timers, to see what they think before charging ahead.

Ultimately, if you do decide to apply yourself, you will likely achieve some partial victories that make the block a bit quieter and less rank while leaving the businesses basically intact. In the process you'll get to know your neighbors, and maybe you'll learn something about how the city works that could be useful for other local projects—like maybe planting some more trees on the block or organizing a block party. Remember: No one in New York has a completely peaceful living situation, not even the very rich or very famous. Meditate on that when you are feeling pissed off.

Or consider investing in those quadruple-paned soundproof (and smell-proof) windows; they might be worth the expense in terms of not losing your mind over this stuff.

With sympathy,
Jake

Dear Jake,

I work the early shift at my job, so I get out around 3 P.M. My walk back to the subway takes me right past a big public high school, which releases its students around the same time. Huge groups of kids block both sides of the street, and sometimes, when you try to squeeze past, they get really rowdy and yell stuff like "Look at this hipster!" (Okay, sometimes they don't say hipster—they say fag, or motherfucker, or a whole list of teenage insults I don't even understand.) Once, I turned around to look at the kid who was yelling and another one actually knocked my baseball cap off my head. I've never been punched or anything, but some days I feel like it's close to that.

There is a race thing going on here. These kids are mostly black and Latino, and I'm white. I'm sure that makes me more of a target in their eyes. All I want to do is get to the subway without getting smacked around or yelled at; what can I do?

Sincerely,
Bullied by Kids

———————————

Dear BBK,

This letter really takes me back to my own high school days. Stuyvesant, the city's premier public school for nerds, was on First Avenue and Fifteenth Street at the time, and Washington Irving, which was one of the toughest high schools in Manhattan, was just a few blocks west. Whenever the L train broke down, we'd have to walk to Union Square to catch the F, and that meant dodging through a minefield of tough miscreants who loved nothing more than pushing a nerd up against a car, stealing his backpack, or just randomly punching him in the head for sport.

Sometimes they didn't even wait for us to come to them. I remember being in shop class one day, gazing idly out the window toward Stuyvesant Park. It was around lunchtime, and suddenly hundreds of Stuyvesant kids were streaming out of the park, pursued by what looked like a barbarian horde of Washington Irving kids. There were several brutal beatdowns that day, my friend, and it was never clear what sparked the melee. In retrospect, it was probably just normal class and race antagonism, and the general loathing the Washington Irving kids harbored for the Stuyvesant kids, who certainly carried a condescending attitude toward them. Not me, of course.

Back then, as a skinny fourteen-year-old, I did everything I could to avoid getting jumped, including *not* leaving at 3 P.M., when most of those kids were getting out of school. It was easy enough to linger for a while hanging out with friends or doing homework, and by 5 P.M., rush hour was starting and I knew there'd be more people on the train (not that it always helped). I also detoured a block or two out of their way, and I deliberately avoided carrying anything that looked too inviting to steal—JanSport backpacks and North Face jackets were the hot items at the time.

Do I recommend you act this paranoid? Absolutely not. You're an adult, and the city is about ten times safer than it was when I was a kid. There's much less tolerance of lawlessness, and that means that while I see kids getting rowdy, I rarely see the outright thuggery that was so routine back then. Most of the time, if you walk straight ahead, stepping boldly, with your head held high, the worst you're going to get is a little smack talk, which is actually good for you because it will toughen you up and make you realize that the opinions of fifteen-year-olds are irrelevant to your self-esteem.

Of course, you have to be the final judge on what is safe. If you can't pass through a crowd without elbowing the kids aside, it's probably worth it to detour across the street. Even today, I never put myself within punching distance of crowds of rowdy teenagers, because you never know which one of them is stupid enough to want to prove something to his friends by stabbing a stranger in the carotid artery and film him bleeding out on Third Avenue for massive WorldStar or YouTube virality. Likewise, steering clear of groups of teenagers congregating under scaffolds and in other secluded areas is just common sense, as the best protection from teenage bad behavior is the presence of other adults. Remember: The biggest danger is not to you, it's to other kids, like young, vulnerable, underweight Jake Dobkin. So please keep your eyes open for bullying or robbery and call the police if you see it happening.

And don't get too angry at these children. New York provides fairly limited options for afternoon activities at most schools, and if your parents work, that means the hours between 3 and 6 p.m. can be unstructured. This is when teenagers are going to get in trouble with their undeveloped brains. In the old days, we had cheap pool halls and arcades to go to, but sadly, most of these have closed—victims of rising rents—so some kids just wind up goofing off with their friends in public spaces such as city sidewalks. Perhaps you can even recall engaging in similar public tom-foolery in your youth? Unless the parents have the wherewithal to get the kid into some kind of organized sport, hanging out on the streets with their friends is probably the most natural and safe place for them to be. There is safety in numbers, and it's good for young people to socialize instead of being latchkey kids returning to an apartment alone. Do not mistake a little juvenile rowdiness for criminality—this is a mistake the police often make with minority kids, and it means they get harassed and arrested far more often than white kids doing the exact same stuff.

I want to discuss for a moment why you often see crowds of black and Latino students congregating outside schools. Where are the white and Asian kids? First, these kids are much more likely to be attending better-funded institutions with after-school programs, so they're less likely to be out on the street. Second, you probably remember seeing them less because you don't feel as scared of white and Asian kids—that's a racist selection bias. And third, New York has one of the most segregated school systems in America, partially due to the residential segregation created by high housing prices, but also because black and Latino students lack the guidance and test prep that allow white and Asian kids to get into specialized schools like Stuyvesant.

I'm not sure you'd be safer if the crowds of kids you pass each day were more diverse. After all, if you put enough 15-year-old kids together, some of them will always do some stupid shit. But I think it would at least reduce some of the tension; a lot of the resentment these kids feel surely comes from knowing that they are crowded into minority schools in disadvantaged communities and that the people in the surrounding neighborhoods are scared of them. Likewise, improving access to after-school programs would go a long way to clearing rowdy teenagers from the streets.

Integrating and improving our public schools will take time, but you don't have to wait for that to happen to feel less scared of these kids. Consider two ideas: taking a self-defense class and volunteering to mentor local youths. The first will give you the skills you need to defend yourself, and the second will teach you that these kids aren't to be feared. Helping them, whether through homework tutoring or taking part in the Big Brothers Big Sisters program, will make you less scared and subliminally racist, and it will help them become more productive members of our diverse city.

Be brave!
Jake

Dear Jake,

I've got a problem: I'm poor. Not starving or homeless poor, but poor enough that just making the rent every month and paying for the necessities pretty much takes my whole paycheck. This is a consequence of my job, which I love—I work at an environmental not-for-profit. I feel like we're doing good work, making New York a cleaner, healthier place, and I like my coworkers and boss. What's begun to bug me, though, is going out with all my college friends who work in for-profit industries like finance and law. They always want to hit the fancy new restaurants and bars and then split the bill.

I do love my friends; they're good people and I know they're not trying to make me uncomfortable, but they are. What should I do?

Sincerely,
Poor Polly

———————————

Dear PP,

One of the positive things about New York is you get to meet so many interesting, successful people. This is also one of the negative things, because there is a high likelihood that at least half, and sometimes, as in your case, most of your friends will be making more money than you. This can either be a cause for unhappiness, or, as we will discuss, an opportunity to reevaluate what you consider important in life.

First, though, let's deal with going out to eat. In your twenties in New York, this is the most popular method of socializing, and it gets expensive fast when drinks are ten or fifteen dollars each and a "small plate" with three meatballs costs twenty dollars. If you want to keep going out with your friends, you could take the lead and suggest cheaper places—there are still dive bars in most neighborhoods, and cheap, excellent ethnic restaurants, mostly in the outer boroughs. Your friends may appreciate your hustle and creativity in finding new places, and you'll have the satisfaction of not being bankrupt at the end of the night.

Or, if they really insist on going out to the fancy places, just make it clear that you can't afford to go. This requires getting real with your friends, but I doubt it will surprise them—they know where you work. If they're friends worth having, they'll either treat you or agree to alter the plans. There are so many fun things to do in New York that don't cost anything: the free nights at our local museums, the outdoor concerts in summer, just hanging out and having a picnic in the park. I wouldn't be surprised if some of your friends would actually prefer doing that stuff—high-end boozing gets really dull after a year or two.

If they're not receptive to your suggestions, you might consider asking yourself whether these are friends you want to have. New York gives you plenty of opportunities to make new acquaintances and then turn those acquaintances into friends. Take those coworkers you like. They're also making the same amount of money as you, and they might be more fun to hang out with. Psychologists say it's much easier to feel relaxed and happy when you are surrounded by people in the same income level as you. Perhaps adding a few friends in your own tax bracket would add some happiness and variety to your life.

But let's say you want to keep some of these well-off friends, because you like them or because they're genuinely good people with whom you feel a true connection. How can you do it without feeling miserable? I've actually had this experience myself. My best friend, who I grew up with in Park Slope, started an internet company that sold for millions, and overnight he became quite rich. At first, I did feel a little uncomfortable—he bought a house in the Hamptons, a nice car, and was suddenly taking vacations I could never afford. I knew, though, that he remained the same good guy he was before, and I didn't want the money to spoil our friendship, so I had to change the way I thought about things.

This started with me really meditating on my values. I'd already been reading a lot of Buddhist and Stoic texts—two ancient traditions that argue materialism is a detriment to happiness and that acquisitiveness or jealousy is a sign of an unquiet mind. From then on, whenever I felt unhappy or uncomfortable about my friend's success, I asked myself, "Why does this make you feel bad?" Usually, after thinking about it for a while, I discovered that deep down I still had the idea that to be truly happy or successful I needed to be rich, and that if I wasn't, I'd failed in some way. Then I meditated some more on where this pernicious idea came from, and that led me to a fairly obvious conclusion.

It came from growing up in New York, steeped in the status-obsessed media we have here and consuming it unconsciously from a very young age. Even those of you who arrived later can't help but be exposed and eventually contaminated by the stuff you see online, on TV, in magazines, and on billboards: pictures and stories about the rich, beautiful, and famous. Even if you consciously reject these values, as I was taught to do while growing up in socialist Park Slope, they still seep into a deep level of your brain, and it takes a lot of work to realize they're down there and release them.

That's why having a rich friend is such a wonderful opportunity: It forced me to recognize these toxic values and face them. Once I did, I was able to set some simple boundaries, like only going out to the fancy restaurants once in a while, and deciding that I could spend time at my friend's house in the Hamptons, but when I did, I'd always be a good guest and try to bring a nice bottle of wine and clean up after myself. Ten years later, I've still got the same best friend, and I think our friendship is stronger than it was before, because I know it's based on mutual respect and not on status or money.

There are other exercises you can practice to make yourself feel better. For instance, when you ride the subway, take a look around: I guarantee that you'll see plenty of people who appear to have even less money than you do (and plenty who appear to have more). Instead of feeling bad about your relative poverty compared to your friends, accept that you are just an average New Yorker doing the best you can, and feel connected to your fellow citizens through this knowledge. Recognize that if worth is based on how much money you have, by definition, most of your fellow

New Yorkers should be miserable because very few people in the city are rich. But, of course, most people are not miserable; they've either decided or just subconsciously realized that a lot of money is not essential to happiness, and human worth should not be judged based on the contents of your savings account.

I don't want to be a Pollyanna here—I recognize that New York is an expensive place to live, and living paycheck to paycheck is extremely stressful. But as we've discussed before, the reason you've chosen that stress is because you believe the payoff is worth it: that living in the greatest city in the world is worth the pain. Keep that in mind as you move forward, and do what you can to reduce the discomfort and increase the joy of living here. You've already got a meaningful job that gives you real satisfaction—now work on making sure you've got the right friends to share inspiring, fulfilling experiences with and the right values to guide you.

I think, after a period of time, you'll realize that how successful or unsuccessful your friends are, or you are, is something that ceases to bother you as much as it once did.

To happiness,
Jake

CHAPTER 6

How to Live Like a New Yorker

Questions

Whoever is born in New York is ill-equipped to deal with any other city: all other cities seem, at best, a mistake, and, at worst, a fraud. No other city is so spitefully incoherent.

—JAMES BALDWIN

Dear Jake,

So, last night I went out drinking with some friends on Smith Street, and after several hours, it was closing time and I had to get back to my apartment in Park Slope. I knew the F train was going to take forever after midnight, and I didn't feel like paying for a cab, so I just decided to walk. I'm a big guy and, anyway, walking through Gowanus at night isn't as dangerous as it used to be.

By the time I got to the Third Street Bridge, I really had to pee. If you've been down there, you know there's nothing around for several blocks, and I knew I was never going to make it home, so I ducked into the parking lot of the Whole Foods, unzipped, and peed right into the Gowanus Canal.

So, as I'm finishing up, I hear, out of nowhere, a voice shouting, "I'm calling the cops!" I don't know if it was a security guard at the supermarket, or someone walking by, or what, but I took off and didn't stop running until I got to Fourth Avenue.

My question: Is it morally wrong to pee outside when there's no other choice?

Best,
Pissing Pete in Park Slope

Dear PPIPS,

I say you did nothing wrong! We New Yorkers have made a peculiar compromise: We have refused to build anything close to the number of public bathrooms the city requires, but when we spot one of the many public pissers that policy decision produces, we usually look the other way, or point and laugh, but rarely actually call the cops. This is because every longtime New Yorker—man or woman, rich or poor—has been in the same situation at least once.

Historically, the NYPD has taken a hardline approach to public urination, especially in poor neighborhoods with tougher enforcement of quality of life crimes. Getting caught pissing outside in Bed-Stuy or the South Bronx could mean a misdemeanor charge, a night languishing in Central Booking, and a criminal record. Recently, the city council, recognizing that the effect of these statutes was disproportionately falling on minorities and the impoverished, passed a law that encouraged the police to treat the crime as a civil violation, which means the perp generally receives only a ticket and a fifty-dollar fine.

So, there was no need to run—unless you were carrying drugs or had an outstanding warrant. The worst that would've happened to you was a ticket and/or an embarrassing lecture by the responding officers. But, given that you were relieving yourself into the most polluted canal in the United States, and probably *improving* the water quality with the addition of your urine, my guess is they would've let you off scot-free.

Not all public urination is a victimless crime. Peeing on someone's stoop or car is what we natives refer to as a "dick move," and, obviously, peeing on a subway car or platform creates disgusting work for the MTA sanitation workers. So, if you must pee in public, be considerate and direct your stream into a sewer grate, or at least onto a square of street pavement that will eventually be cleaned by the rain. You often see parents with little kids pointing them toward fire hydrants or between cars—follow their lead.

Or, better yet, pee before you leave the bar! If you forget, try to avail yourself of the many available private bathrooms that the city has to offer. Even in Gowanus, at night, there are several bars open along Third Avenue, and in most neighborhoods, you have plenty of restaurants and Starbuckses you can duck into for free. Once you live here long enough, you'll develop a mental map of the closest and best bathroom in every neighborhood. My favorites are the hotel lobby bathrooms in Midtown. As long as you don't appear homeless and act like you know where you're going, you can stroll right in, and they are all immaculately clean and private.

A final thought: When it comes to public restrooms, New York is an outlier in its cohort of large, wealthy cities. In Europe, public bathrooms are common and are often operated as a business; the proprietor collects a small entrance fee, and in return keeps the place clean and off-limits to disreputable types. We could easily follow a similar model here, utilizing the bathrooms at subway stations that were closed in the 1970s but still exist.

This won't happen unless the public demands it, though. If you're not too squeamish, consider advancing the idea the next time your local council representative does a round of community budgeting in which they solicit ideas from the public on how to allocate building funds in the district.

In solidarity,
Jake

N.B.: Should you find yourself in this situation frequently, there are several websites and apps that recommend available bathrooms around NYC.

Dear Jake,

Every morning, on the way to work, I buy my coffee and cigarettes from a bodega that looks straight out of the 1970s. Literally—the signage is at least forty years old, and some of the cans of soup in the back aisle look to be about the same age. My question is: How does this place stay in business when all the other old stores are gone? Is there some secret that I don't understand?

Sincerely,
Pack-a-Day

———————————

Dear PAD,

You really need to quit smoking. It's suicidal, makes your clothes stink, and increasingly relegates you to the margins of society as more and more places ban it. Did you know that smoking is illegal now in all of our New York City parks? Soon it'll be banned even in private apartments, and you'll have to go outside in the dead of winter to get your fix. Better to start preparing now—the city makes free quitting kits with nicotine gum available through 311, and they can also hook you up with counseling services to get this deadly monkey off your back.

But your question was about your local bodega. Interestingly, your smoking is one of the reasons it is still in business, as cigarettes are a high-profit-margin product. They don't take up a ton of space and if, as at many bodegas, the owner is trucking them up from Virginia and not paying the New York State stamp tax, they can be the most lucrative items for sale in the store. There are other high-profit items with a fast turnover, like beer, that can balance out a lot of stuff in the store that hardly moves at all, like those dusty Campbell's soup cans in the back.

Even with these lucrative items, real bodegas are becoming an endangered species in New York, as competition from national chains like

7-Eleven and drugstores like Rite Aid with convenience aisles continually expand to new neighborhoods. Then there are the more upscale "green markets" that sell produce and prepared foods—all of these businesses can pay more rent than the humble old-time bodega, and so, as their leases end, many of the iconic red-and-yellow awnings are disappearing.

The word *bodega* means "warehouse" in Spanish. When Spanish-speaking immigrants first came to New York in the early decades of the twentieth century, they brought with them a tradition of small neighborhood stores selling a variety of things: canned food, newspapers, cigarettes, candy, etc. Later, after Prohibition was lifted in 1933, these stores began to stock beer, and around the same time, as refrigeration technology gained widespread use, these stores also began selling fresh foods—fruit, vegetables, milk, eggs, and even prepared items like the venerable bacon, egg & cheese on a roll that many New Yorkers eat every day.

Though we still use the word *bodega*, it's a myth that all bodega owners are Spanish-speaking Puerto Ricans or Dominicans. It really varies by area and tends to match the population of the surrounding neighborhood. Running a bodega is a difficult job with long hours, and as each successive generation of immigrants arrive, some of the owners sell out and move on to easier professions.

To the extent your local place has survived, it may have some special advantages. Perhaps the owner was smart or lucky enough to buy the building back in the bad old days of the 1970s, when many landlords were willing to part with them cheaply, or perhaps the bodega has a lucrative side business selling something else out of the back of the store. Plenty of bodegas in the old days were sustained by dealing marijuana or cocaine, although this has become rarer as drug delivery services have grown in popularity over the last fifteen years. There are still other illegal items, like khat, a plant whose dried leaves produce an amphetamine-like effect when chewed, which can be found at many Arab- and African-owned bodegas.

We natives are willing to look the other way on any minor illegality because we realize the important role bodegas play in the community. They're not just stores, they're also community centers where longtime residents gather to discuss the news and connect with one another. They're de facto post offices where you can have your Amazon deliveries left when you're at work, and key-holders who can keep your spare set for when you inevitably lose yours or have to leave a key for your in-laws or (more likely) Airbnb guests to get in. The bodegas can do this stuff because they're usually family owned, with the same people working every day for many years. That gives them a connection to the community that a Rite Aid, with its high-turnover minimum-wage workers, will never have.

Another thing bodegas have over those fluorescent-lit mega stores: bodega cats. Since bodegas were largely built on the ground floors of old buildings, they were impossible to fully guard against mice coming in from the outside—those old brownstones and tenements simply have too many holes in them. So, wishing to avoid infestation, bodega owners usually adopt a stray cat and let them roam freely through the store and basement, keeping the place vermin-free and providing a popular mascot for the store. Though this is in violation of the city's health code, somehow the cats have survived—many are quite popular with the local children who stop in just to pet the cat and not to buy anything.

How can you support your local bodega, besides continuing to buy your filthy cigarettes and other sundry items there instead of a corporate chain? One political suggestion: For about thirty years, our city council members have been trying to pass a Small Business Jobs Survival Act, which would force landlords to write at least ten year leases, with renewal options. So far, the bill has stalled because of opposition from the developer interests, but recently, as the last two real-estate booms have kicked rents into the stratosphere and accelerated the die-off of small businesses into something like a mass extinction, there seems to be a greater chance of passing it than ever before.

The next time you vote for your local representative, make sure he or she supports this common-sense bill.

Cordialmente,
Jake

Dear Jake,

I live alone in a studio in Hell's Kitchen and I work in Midtown. Life is pretty good! I can walk to work, my cubicle and apartment both have decent light, and I have a bunch of friends to go out with on weekends. But during the week, I find myself a little lonely. I go to the gym, make dinner, and then usually watch TV until bed. I'm thinking that a pet would be good company, but I'm not sure whether to get a cat or a dog. What do you recommend?

Yours truly,
Prospective Pet Parent

Dear PPP,

You should get a cat. They make wonderful companions, do well in small apartments, and don't require a ton of attention during the day. Getting a dog, especially without fully considering the consequences and profound impact on your life and habits, would be a terrible mistake. Dog ownership in NYC is an advanced-level project, something you do in your thirties or forties when you've given up on the rest of your dreams and need something else to fill the time.

I got my first cat when I was twenty-seven. My wife and I were living in a small apartment down on Thompson Street, and we named the cat after the block. He was perfect: a dark black Persian whose favorite activities were sitting on your chest and purring, or falling asleep on your feet while you watched TV. Even though he had a whole host of health problems that come with being a purebred cat (irritable bowel syndrome, missing tear ducts, regular semi-fatal hairball attacks), he still was easier to take care of than a dog. As long as he had water and cat food, and you cleaned out his litterbox daily, he was happy.

Thompson lived to the ripe old cat age of thirteen (which is like 130 in Persian years) and passed away just recently. We're planning, after an appropriate period of mourning, to get a new cat, and the only change we're going to make is adopting one at a shelter. Mixed-breed shelter cats are generally more durable than finicky purebreds and, given the environmental toxins cats are exposed to in New York (giant roaches, mice loaded up with urban germs, etc.), durability is very important. It's also a big, big mitzvah to save a cat from a shelter, particularly the older cats that have a tougher time getting adopted.

Contrast my cat experience to the week I've just spent with my in-laws' dog, Charlie. They're in town for the holidays and, as I avoid Midtown like the plague during these weeks, Charlie and I are often home while the rest of the family goes to see the Rockefeller Center Christmas Tree or *The Nutcracker* at Lincoln Center. This has given me plenty of time to study the habits of a dog in the city, which seem to involve: 1) begging to be taken out for a walk, 2) being out for a walk, 3) resting for about fifteen minutes, then begging for treats, and 4) either going out for another walk or peeing on the floor in protest. Charlie is a great dog, by the way—charming personality, so cute and fluffy that people routinely stop me while I walk him to pet his coat—but this is just the way dogs are built.

Then there are the actual walks. It's fun to get outside, and one definite plus is you get to meet all the other people in the neighborhood with canines, but after a few trips, especially in the freezing cold, it begins to lose its magic. Especially when your dog wants to stop and pee on every single pole on every single block (where do they store up that much pee?) and has a pathological fear of many elements of the urban street scene: sidewalk grates, those metal basement doors, and most other dogs. This seems to be matched by his predilection to investigate and occasionally try to eat every kind of garbage he can get his paws on.

Oh, I forgot to mention the poop. Cat poop is generally contained and easily handled—cleaning out a litter box is unpleasant, but if you do it every day, it takes about thirty seconds with a plastic scooper. Cleaning up dog-doo is a whole different magnitude of disgusting. First, you have wait until he finds the perfect spot, which can take, like, an hour of investigating. Then, once he does his business, you have to clean it up, which involves placing one of those thin poop-baggies on your hand and picking up the still-warm droppings, flipping it inside out, and then finding a place to quickly deposit the bag, which is more difficult than it sounds because most people on the block do not want you dropping poop in their garbage cans.

My time with Charlie lasts just a few days a year, but it's more than enough to convince me that I'd never be able to handle the commitment of dog ownership. Between the constant walking, the danger of the dog wrecking your apartment if he's left alone too long, and the prospect of picking up poop multiple times daily for fifteen or twenty years, no way. Kids at least grow out of diapers after a few years, but having a dog is like having a baby that never grows up. I know, angry dog people reading this essay, you believe the positives of dog ownership outweigh these negatives! But to the young New Yorker starting out with a first pet, cats are a far safer route to take. If you are a prospective dog owner and don't believe me, at least volunteer to pet sit a friend's pooch for a week before you plunge ahead—or better yet, host a dog through one of the shelter foster programs. You'll quickly discover if you have what it takes.

There are also the costs to consider. A sturdy shelter cat requires very little: cat food, litter box supplies, an occasional vet visit. I have a friend who adopted two shelter cats and then didn't take them to the vet for fifteen years, and they both continue to thrive in perfect health. Contrast that with a dog's costs. Since they're frequently outside, they're going to need rounds of shots to protect them from communicable diseases, and then they'll need regular checkups every time they start throwing up from something they ate off the sidewalk. Then there are the pet-sitting and dog-walking fees, doggie daycare, costs of doggie outfits for winter (four boots and a coat add up!), grooming, etc. This is a major investment that you should talk to your accountant about in advance.

The most important thing is that you approach this decision with the right attitude: Pet adoption is a serious responsibility that should not be viewed as a way to fill some black hole of urban loneliness deep in your soul. For that, you need friends, activities, and therapy. No, pet adoption should be seen from the zen point of view as an opportunity to provide care to another sentient being, and thereby expand your heart. If you're not ready for that level of giving, proceed no further—this is not an iPad or piece of exercise equipment that you can, in good conscience, return if you realize it doesn't produce the happiness that you thought it would.

Proceed with caution,
Jake

N.B.: You should also check your lease to make sure it allows animals. If not, ask the building managers, because they sometimes make exceptions for cats or small dogs. And know the law: According to NYC.gov, "a dog license costs $8.50 per year for spayed or neutered dogs or $34 per year for non-spayed or neutered dogs. Dog licenses may be purchased or renewed for one to five years." Finally, get those implantable RFID tags for any animal you adopt; they can be a lifesaver if they ever get lost.

Dear Jake,

The other night was a hot one, and a friend and I decided to go sit in the playground across the street from my apartment to enjoy the breeze and talk. After about an hour, two police officers suddenly appeared and demanded to see our identification. We showed it to them, and after a few minutes, they pulled out their pad and wrote us a pink ticket, which costs up to $300—apparently, we were there outside of park hours. I feel like this is really unfair: The playground was unlocked, no one was using it, and we weren't drinking—we were just sitting there. Are natives aware that this kind of thing is a ticketable offense? Are there other crimes I might be accidentally committing that I'm not aware of?

Sincerely,
The Law Won

Dear TLW,

Look on the bright side: Until fairly recently, your night could have ended with a much bigger fine, and even an arrest, depending on how the police officer was feeling about you. Back in the bad old days, when the city was much more dangerous, the "broken windows" policing strategy meant little infractions like this were treated as very big deals. If you didn't have ID on you, or were young and black, or were in a poorer neighborhood, a minor violation could turn into a couple of days in a holding cell before you even got to see a judge, and then up to fifteen days of jail time if you couldn't pay the fine.

By the end of the Bloomberg administration, this approach to crime was already on the wane—unconstitutional "stop and frisks" declined as a result of lawsuits against the city, and as crime dropped to historic lows, the need to dragnet hundreds of people each day into the system using petty violations came to be seen as an unnecessary, even racist, overreach by the NYPD. This new understanding was ratified as law in 2016, as the mayor and city council passed a package of bills reducing the use of criminal summons and possible jail time, lowering fines, and allowing community service in lieu of cash payment. This affected a variety of offenses—consumption of alcohol in public (the most common violation by far), disorderly conduct, bicycling on sidewalks, trespassing, possession of marijuana, making "unreasonable noise," public urination, and your crime: failing to comply with signs in a park.

(A note on the language we use to describe crimes in New York City: Violations are similar to traffic tickets, in that they are generally punishable by fines, and don't create a criminal record, but can lead to up to fifteen days of jail time. Some violations don't come with automatic fines that can be paid by mail or online, and you have to waste a full day of your life going to court to get them dismissed or paid. Misdemeanors are more serious crimes generally punishable by up to a year in jail on Rikers Island, and felonies are the most serious crimes—the rapes, assaults, and murders that can lead to long prison sentences upstate.)

It is literally impossible to grow up in New York and not commit several of these violations. I just think of my late teenage years—in one night, we might have consumed 40s on a stoop (because we couldn't get into any bars, but bodegas would sell us beer), then hung out in a park after hours, gotten loud and disorderly arguing about something dumb, and then capped off the night with some celebratory public urination. I never got a ticket for any of it, because even in those days, white kids in richer neighborhoods were treated with an extraordinarily unfair degree of tolerance by the cops, while poorer kids in minority neighborhoods would've found themselves up against the hood of a police car for doing exactly the same stuff.

I'll tell you the story of the one time I did catch a violation. This was on a Sunday morning, in a part of Bushwick that was still very industrial, back in my early twenties. No one was around, and I was biking here and there, taking some pictures of graffiti and generally enjoying a nice spring day. Coming up a block, I spied a truck taking up the entire street, and I veered on to the sidewalk to go around it. Of course, right on the other side of the truck was a police van, which proceeded to stop me. Like you, I explained I didn't mean to break the law, that I hadn't endangered anyone, and it was really the truck that was acting dangerously by blocking traffic. The eight officers who were in the van listened politely, took my ID, and then wrote me a pink ticket—the whole process probably took twenty minutes. When I complained bitterly about this to a criminal lawyer I know, she laughed and said, "You were in Bushwick; this happens to people there every single day."

She's right. Even today, enforcement of all the minor violations is still tilted to the highly policed neighborhoods. It might be intentional NYPD strategy, as a leftover from the "stop-and-frisk" days, or it could be the simple byproduct of having a lot of officers on the streets in these neighborhoods looking for stuff to do, like trying to fill the monthly ticket quotas that the police commissioners have always denied exist. One small but often-overlooked upside of gentrification of these neighborhoods is that the police exercise more caution if they feel the population is richer and whiter, and this can have the effect of protecting all residents from ticketing or arrest over petty stuff like this.

For most people, getting slapped with a violation every ten years is the price of going about your business in New York. As we discussed earlier in this chapter, with the lack of public bathrooms in this city, there will probably be at least one time you are going to find yourself needing to pee outside. You will *almost* certainly not get caught, so do what you gotta do. The other offenses are easily avoided—if you are forced to take your bike on the sidewalk, for instance, simply dismount and walk. If you want to hang out in a park at night, simply check the signs to see what time the park closes (sometimes it's "dusk," sometimes 1 A.M.). Don't drink outside, or if you do, stick to safer spaces like your own stoop. Don't smoke weed outside your apartment—that smell travels, and it's an easy violation for the police to write once they spot you.

If you do find yourself confronted by the police over a violation, simply be polite, say as little as possible, and accept the ticket without much of a fight. Once they start writing it, there's almost no way to get them to stop, so don't waste too much of your breath. It just annoys them and gives them reason to think of other things they can bust you for. Always carry ID—the most common reason for a trip to the station is getting popped by the cops without it, which gives them a reason to take you in until you can prove who you are. Finally, if you are given the option, just pay the fine by mail and be done with it—you may win in court, but you'll still have lost that time at work, and it'll be at most a washout in terms of cost.

This advice does not apply to people in some specific groups: Illegal immigrants and people in jobs that require a background check should consult with a lawyer before proceeding to pay the ticket or going to court. But for everyone else, congratulations: You've just received a real New York merit badge, and you have a story you can tell about the time you ran afoul of the law and survived. That's definitely a key ingredient in any street cred you can lay claim to later on.

Fight the power,
Jake

Dear Jake,

I've got a problem: Ever since I got my own apartment in New York (a one-bedroom in Harlem), every friend, relative, and old college acquaintance I've known in my life seems to be emailing and asking if they can crash at my place during their trip to New York. Which, if any, of these people must I play host to? Do I have to take them around or can I just give them a guide book and send them on their way? Can I ask for anything in return? After all, I'm saving them like $200 a night on a hotel room by letting them sleep on my pull-out couch.

Sincerely,
Hassled Host

Dear HH,

How lucky you are to not only live in the greatest city on Earth, but to also have an apartment large enough to host visitors and have a multitude of people who want to spend time with you! Let us meditate on that for a moment before we proceed, and then show compassion to at least some of these visitors, who are cursed to live out their days somewhere that is not New York.

Of course we cannot take pity on everyone; you are not running a hotel. The unofficial rule in New York is that hosting obligations are limited to immediate family and close friends—anyone else is at your discretion. That means those college buddies you haven't seen in five years may need to rent a hotel room or Airbnb. You can help them by recommending a few places and offering to meet them for dinner or a drink, but you have no obligation to let them sleep in your home.

How do you communicate this politely? Time for the white lie of your choice! Maybe you have a cousin coming to visit that week who has already booked the couch, or the place is set to be fumigated, or you are scheduled to give a big presentation that week at work and need quiet to prepare. This

Top Ten Places That Real New Yorkers Won't Go Willingly

1 **TIMES SQUARE, PARTICULARLY ON NEW YEAR'S EVE.** You can go once to appreciate why you should never do it again, and then avoid the whole area for ten or twenty years.

2 **STATUE OF LIBERTY.** I'm guessing at least half of all native New Yorkers have never been there. You can see it fine from the Staten Island Ferry, and who wants to wait in that line for the tourist boat?

3 **EMPIRE STATE BUILDING.** If you want to see the skyline, you can do that for free from the Brooklyn Heights Promenade, the walkway on the Brooklyn Bridge, or for the price of a subway fare from the Smith–Ninth Street Station on the F, or via the Roosevelt Island Tramway.

4 **THE SEPTEMBER 11TH MEMORIAL.** To the natives, it's sacred and painful ground, and we don't need to see people smiling for selfies in front of the fountains.

5 **MUSEUMS ON WEEKENDS.** It's far more pleasant to cut out of work early on a weekday and go when they're empty; this also goes for the High Line.

6   **PENN STATION.** This inscrutable rat warren is at the very bottom of any New Yorker's list of transportation hubs because of its crowds, low ceilings, dreadful restrooms, and perennial delays. Natives do their best to avoid it by picking up LIRR trains at Atlantic Terminal in Brooklyn and Jamaica Station in Queens.

7   **PORT AUTHORITY BUS TERMINAL.** A near tie with Penn Station for "worst way to enter or leave New York City," and famous for its filth and human misery, it has largely been made obsolete by the discount bus lines based in Chinatown and outside the Javits Center—at least for intercity travel.

8   **FIVE-STAR RESTAURANTS.** These are for visiting tourists and businesspeople with expense accounts—the locals prefer not to spend $500 per person for fifteen courses of barely edible art displays.

9   **SOHO.** This neighborhood has devolved into an outdoor mall with all the charm of the Thirty-fourth Street shopping strip, and its crowded and overpriced luxury-goods stores have largely been abandoned by longtime residents.

10 **NEW JERSEY.** The ancient rivalry remains strong, and despite its cheaper housing opportunities, there is no indignity worse for a native than surrendering his New York citizenship and moving across the river.

route will be less hurtful than the truth, which is that they are not close enough friends to merit couch status. The only downside is that, if they find out you are lying, they will have hurt feelings, so be sure to pick a simple, solid lie and stick to it. Remember, though, it is their unfair request that put you in this situation, so don't feel too bad about making up an excuse.

For close family and friends, unfortunately, you have an obligation to let them stay on your couch, if you are at all able. Unless you're scheduled to take the LSATs the next morning, there are very few reasons that will get you out of hosting a brother, sister, parent, or best friend. That does not mean you are responsible for escorting them around our metropolis during the day—you have a job and a life, and good boundaries are essential to any relationship. Sure, reserve one day to show them around your favorite New York spots, but let them hit Times Square on their own.

When you do take them around, make sure you pick stuff off the beaten track that they'll remember long after they leave the city. Places that impress themselves on the senses, such as a walk around Chinatown, lying in the grass at the Sheep Meadow in Central Park, or restaurants that are truly memorable—pizza at Lucali or drinks at the King Cole Bar. Make sure they walk around at least one neighborhood in the outer boroughs besides your own and get there on the subway, which is a quintessential part of our city. You want to show them *your* New York and give them a sense of why you're willing to tough it out here.

During your time in New York, you will probably give a lot more than you get out of these times playing host. It's unlikely that you'll be going to Cleveland or Buffalo any time soon to get an opportunity for these guests to reciprocate, and that's fine. That is the price you pay for the privilege of living here. There is good karma in this, and you will be rewarded will loyal, grateful friends. Of course, don't let anyone abuse the privilege—at the very least they should pay for a meal or a nice bottle of wine as a thank you gift for your services.

To friendship,
Jake

Dear Jake,

The other day it was raining, and I was too lazy to go out to get lunch, so I ordered from my local cheap Chinese restaurant. When the guy came to deliver it, I gave what I considered to be a generous tip on the credit card slip—two dollars on a ten-dollar order. And yet the delivery guy gave me kind of a grumbling look and didn't say thank you. What's up with that?

Yours truly,
Dissed Tipper

Dear DT,

Yes, you made two mistakes: You under tipped and you didn't give the tip in cash. The rule for food delivery tips in New York is three dollars or 20 percent of the order, whichever is more, up to a maximum of twenty dollars. If it's raining, you're going to need to go up from there—on your ten-dollar order, I would've tipped at least four dollars.

Why? First, delivering food on a bike is one of the most difficult, dangerous jobs in all of New York. That's during normal weather—during rain, sleet, or snow, it's even worse. The delivery men are almost always treated as third-party contractors by the restaurants they work for; that means no health insurance if they get hit by a car, and they have to pay for their own bike if it gets stolen while they're coming up to deliver your food.

For this work they receive only the tipped minimum wage, currently $7.50 in New York (though rising to ten dollars in 2020). The law does require them to make at least $3–3.50 in tips per hour, going up to five dollars per hour in 2020, but that means their total income is likely less than $20,000 a year. That's if they even get paid what they are owed— plenty of restaurants rip off their delivery guys in various ways; chief among them is stealing all or a portion of the credit card tip receipts. Remember: These delivery guys are usually undocumented immigrants, so they often feel they can't go to the cops, and their only option when this happens is to tough it out or switch restaurants.

The law in New York is quite clear on this point: Credit card tips are supposed to go, 100 percent, to the delivery guy. Large delivery companies, like Seamless and Grubhub, do perform their obligations, although often it's because they've been targeted by the attorney general for wage violations in the past, or they are trying to avoid an investigation like that in the future. For smaller restaurants, like the Chinese place you ordered from, always tip in cash because you never know if the owner is treating his people right.

Even if you are not sympathetic to the plight of oppressed deliverymen and believe it's your right to leave a low tip or no tip, consider that it might be in your personal interest to tip well. It is very likely that if this is a restaurant you like, you will encounter this deliveryman again, and when you do, you want to be sure your egg drop soup hasn't been spilled all over your spare ribs "by accident." That's just the tip of the iceberg of what a vindictive person with access to your food could get away with. Better to be on the safe side and tip well, and always remember to thank the deliverymen for their hard work.

Bon appetit,
Jake

N.B.: There are so many other situations in which our New York culture requires us to tip. Here are a few of the most important ones with the standard amounts we natives use:

1. **Cabs:** 15 to 20 percent—or higher if he got you there fast or helped with luggage. This includes Lyft and Uber drivers; you can set the tip percentage in your account setup or do it in cash at the end of the ride.
2. **Waitstaff at restaurants:** 20 percent. This used to be 15 percent, but the norm has changed.

3. **Bartenders:** One dollar per beer, two dollars per drink for fancy mixed cocktails (anything more complicated than a gin and tonic) if you're paying in cash, or 20 percent of the bill on credit cards.

4. **Grocery delivery:** Two dollars per bag, up to twenty dollars, and more if you ordered an enormous amount of heavy stuff. And even more if it's a walk-up.

5. **Furniture delivery:** Twenty dollars for one item delivered by two men, ten dollars for each additional man on the team. More if the items are especially unwieldy, like a large couch.

6. **Supers and building staff:** $50 to $250 per year at the holidays depending on size of the building—more if they are very helpful. If you live in a large building with many people working, you need to tip each person you interact with. Usually they will give you a list of names and positions before the holidays, and you can consult the web for correct amounts corresponding to each job.

7. **Dog walkers, regular babysitters, house cleaners, and anyone else working for you regularly throughout the year:** Tip one week's pay and give them a thoughtful card at the end of the year thanking them for their service.

CHAPTER 7

How to Afford Life in New York

Questions

Make your mark in
New York and you are
a made man.

—MARK TWAIN

Dear Jake,

New York City is horribly, diabolically expensive. It's a rare month that I find myself with anything left in my bank account after paying rent. How do you natives survive here, generation after generation, without going broke or moving somewhere cheaper? Do you have any secret knowledge that can help the rest of us?

Sincerely,
Broke in Bushwick

Dear BIB,

New York is expensive for everyone, even natives, but we do have three advantages that you do not: access to cheaper housing, generational knowledge about how to live less expensively, and networks of friends and family to help us find work and survive lean periods of unemployment. Let's consider each separately and see if there are any lessons that a non-native could learn something from.

First, housing. Natives benefit from far higher access to rent-stabilized and rent-controlled apartments passed down from one relative to another. This is often a cause for vociferous complaints from newcomers such as you: "Why does that guy get cheap rent while I have to pay through the nose?" The answer is that person and his forebears built this city and suffered through its bad old days, while you just arrived last month. You have not made the same sacrifices, and thus have not earned the same benefits.

While the vast majority of New Yorkers rent, about a third own their apartments and houses, and for the natives who fall into this category, this real estate is passed down generation after generation. Sometimes grandparents, parents, and grandkids all live together in one house, which not only promotes family cohesion but can also be a great way to avoid paying a lot for rent. Often, the mortgage has been paid off long ago, and the only costs are property taxes (which are low for one- and two-unit houses in New York) and repairs (which can be expensive, but they knew how to build houses back in the day, and the big repair bills don't come around too often).

I actually do this, myself. After my wife and I had our second kid, living in a one-bedroom apartment was no longer cutting it, and I moved back to the Park Slope house I grew up in. My parents generously offered me the top two floors of the house if I'd pay for the renovation and pay them a discounted rent. The deal has worked out well for both of us— they get to see their grandkids every day, have me to take out the garbage, shovel snow, and constantly fix their computers, and I have some built-in babysitting and lower housing costs. It's not for everyone, of course; you ideally want a house or apartment that can be reasonably subdivided and family relationships strong enough to support everyday proximity. But I have several other acquaintances in the neighborhood doing the same thing, because real estate is just too expensive in New York not to use any discount you can find, even if it means moving in with your parents.

Besides marrying a native, is there anything you can learn from this that would benefit your bank balance? How about just moving in with your girlfriend or boyfriend, native or not, and splitting the rent—that's one of the fastest ways to bring down your housing costs. Just be careful, because this is also a huge step that can blow up in your face if you take it before you're both ready. Cohabitate too soon in a relationship, and one of you could be forced to find a new place to live as quickly as possibly under the most wrenching emotional circumstances. A friend of mine once went through a horrible breakup while cohabitating with his ex in a tiny studio apartment—they couldn't get out of their lease for several months, and it was an absolute nightmare for both of them. We'll talk about that more in the next chapter.

If you can, try to find a rent-stabilized apartment; they are fairly common in the outer boroughs, and in some neighborhoods, they are approximately the same cost as market-rate apartments. By renting one, you won't save money immediately, but over time, your rent increases will be kept manageable, and you will be able to stay in New York for as long as you like. If you aren't willing to move to a far-flung neighborhood, consider applying to the monthly affordable housing lotteries the city and state hold, often for apartments in high-demand areas. Though you have to be in a specific income bracket, and it is unlikely that you will win (as it is common for each lottery to get 100,000 or more entrants), it doesn't hurt to try. Call 311 for more information.

Beyond housing, we natives have a few other secrets to living cheaply. First, we don't dine out as much as you do; we tend to eat in with our families and friends. Second, we typically avail ourselves of the local public schools, often through college, so we don't have as many of the expensive student loans you're probably carrying. Third, we use our knowledge of the city to keep our costs down. That can be as simple as avoiding cabs in favor of the subway most of the time, or knowing which supermarkets are total rip-offs and which are actually pretty good deals. Many of us have mastered the art of scraping by in lean times on dollar slices and ramen noodles when necessary. All of this knowledge and more can be yours if you can make a native friend. If not, use your common sense, because no one who isn't sensibly frugal is going to survive here for very long.

Lastly, natives don't just save money, they have more ways to *make* money through their network of local family and friends. Whether that's a job with the city or a local company that your cousin puts you up for, or just good advice about which careers comport well with life here, the informational advantages that come from knowing a lot of people can translate into real dollar benefits. You can replicate this to some extent by getting to know as many people as you can—branch out beyond the group of college and work friends you hang out with now. Get involved in some political-activist groups, an athletic league, a volunteer situation, or any continuing-education class, and watch how quickly your options for work expand.

Knowing a lot of people is particularly helpful when shit hits the fan and you lose a job, get sick, or encounter one of the other calamities most

New Yorkers face after a period of time. When stuff like this happens, we natives are quick to call on our family, whether for a place to stay, help recuperating, or emotional support. A broad network of friends, colleagues, and acquaintances will give you some of the same benefits, and you should try to put one together *before* you need it, because afterward it'll be too late and you'll have to move back home to Peoria to get the support you need.

Remember: Today's natives are just the children or grandchildren of people like you who came here and somehow hacked it. Follow some of this advice, and your descendants will one day think back and say, "Thank God for my grandparents, without whom I'd surely be dying of boredom in the suburbs."

Wishing you success,
Jake

Top Ten Ways to Save Money (Not Previously Mentioned)

1   Buy a monthly MetroCard. Better yet, buy it through your work's transit-pass program, if they offer one, to save almost 50 percent.

2   Apply for (and win) one of the frequent NYC housing lotteries. Go to NYC.gov for more info—it's the next best thing to inheriting a $500-per-month rent-controlled apartment from your grandma.

3   If you live in a small building, offer to handle the trash and shovel the snow for a discount on your rent.

4   Join your local food co-op or CSA and cook at home. You will eat healthier and save money. Plan your fine-dining experiences for Restaurant Week.

5   Make your own coffee at home and work, and prepare your own lunch: Spending twenty dollars a day on this stuff is highly avoidable.

6   So many of the cultural treasures in NYC are available for free at many of our world-class museums; you can also catch most movies for a discounted rate at matinees, and buy half-price tickets for most Broadway shows at TKTS.

7   New York's public libraries are the best in the world, and they also offer free e-books, audiobooks, and streaming movies.

8   Drink at happy hours, or at home, and give up smoking altogether: You already know you should, and a pack of cigs is currently fifteen dollars.

9   Between our city's many amazing discount stores, like Century 21, and our many secondhand marketplaces, like Goodwill, you never have to pay full price for clothing, footwear, furniture, or basically anything else.

10 Quit your gym. If you want to run, use our city's beautiful parks; if you want to swim, try one of the city's rec centers, which beat even the YMCA for cheap memberships.

Dear Jake,

I'm a fellow native New Yorker and, back in 2011, I was in high
school downtown when the Occupy Wall Street Protests broke out
in Zuccotti Park. In my own small way I took part, making signs after
school, hanging out in the park, and going on marches (my parents
wouldn't let me stay overnight). It was a real awakening for me:
from solidarity with other young people, to learning about the way
banks manipulate our economy for their own benefit, to participating
in political action.

Flash forward six years and I'm set to graduate from college,
and my only job offer is . . . from a Wall Street bank. Would I be
a hypocrite to accept this job? Is it wrong to work for an institution
you think is bad for the country?

Sincerely,
Occupied with Wall Street

Dear OWWS,

Wow, how the wheel turns! Everyone is a socialist until they get that first
student loan bill, huh? That said, I think you should take the job. It'll
teach you a number of important lessons about life. To start: The financial
industry, and any particular bank, is not a monolith that can be painted as
wholly good or evil. The industry employs hundreds of thousands of people in New York City, and it makes up about 15 percent of our economy—
that's our largest sector except for real estate—in boom years. Sure, some
Wall Streeters are Gordon Gekko greed machines bent only on profit at
any cost, but most are people just like you and me, trying to get by and
support their families in one of the most expensive cities on Earth.

It would help to know what part of the bank you've been invited to
work for. If you're taking a job in marketing to design better ad campaigns
so people open up savings accounts, I doubt anyone would fault you

morally; any harm that the bank does is simply too far removed from your job. On the other hand, if you are working on a desk that packages shady mortgage-backed securities, which was one of the main causes of the 2008 economic collapse, and later the inspiration for the Occupy movement, you might have more reason to pause. Ask yourself: What are the effects, near and far, of this job on society? Is it an amoral job, like most on Wall Street, in that it's just a gear in the cogs of capitalism, or could it be actually immoral, like knowingly screwing someone—pension fund investors, people looking to buy their first homes, or 401(k) account holders?

Even if it is an evil department, that doesn't mean you need to turn down the job; you still have options. The first is to take the job and do your moral penance outside work—volunteering for a worthy cause, flaying yourself with one of those spike chains that were popular in the Middle Ages, giving money to nonprofits, etc. Wall Street supports many of our city's most important charities in this way. The problem with this approach is that the overall evil your office does might far outweigh any individual good you could do outside of work, and so on balance, you will be making the world a worse place. The second is that working an evil job, surrounded by evil people, tends to make a person evil, and after a few months you might adopt their values and just keep all the cash for yourself.

If it is evil, there's one more way you could take the job without soiling your conscience, and that's by taking the system down from the inside. This is a very difficult road—preserving your own values while surrounded by people who don't share them and slowly gathering information on any shenanigans you observe to later leak to the press or the prosecutors. Remember: If you don't take this job, some other kid will, possibly without your moral compass, so you can make the argument that the world is a better place if you take it first. Even if you're not prepared for full WikiLeaks-style vigilantism, you could simply gum up the works by doing a shitty job (but not so shitty it gets you fired) while using the experience you build up to find a better position somewhere else in due time.

What sort of job would count as "better"? Well, you seem to be an idealistic young person, so the first thing would be a job with purpose, one that's contributing to making the world a better place. The problem is, these jobs tend to pay less compared to finance, and the costs of living in New York make it difficult to follow an idealistic course. A grave danger about going right to Wall Street out of college is that you will adjust your living standards upward so high that you will never be able to feel comfortable living on less, and that will trap you in the industry forever. To combat this, make sure you're living modestly no matter how big your bonus is: Get an apartment with a roommate, and keep most of what you earn in savings so you can, if you choose, eventually transition to a field that pays less but offers more spiritual satisfaction.

What sorts of fields make the world a better place? The helping professions, certainly—teachers, nurses, doctors, therapists. Or not-for-profits doing work in important areas of pressing local or worldwide concern: poverty, environmentalism, or housing. Even banks often have wings that do social lending to charities and pro-human projects, usually to burnish the bank's reputation. It's possible that you could locate such a department in your own company, get a transfer, and find that you can do good while still making a fair amount of money.

Anyway, don't torture yourself. At age twenty-three, you could have a dozen or more jobs in front of you before you retire. The work of your first years out of school is to figure out what's important to you, what isn't, what kind of jobs you like, and which ones you don't. You don't have to save the world right away, and plenty of banking associates figure out after a year that there are ways to apply the analytic skills they learned at their jobs to fields outside of finance. Some of the people you met at Occupy Wall Street in 2011 were current or ex-finance workers who were interested in the movement because it resonated with their own objections to their work.

Who knows, maybe when the next collapse comes, and the next movement rises, you'll be back on the barricades again—older, wiser, and armed with some inside knowledge that can help accomplish some lasting change.

To a more just world,
Jake

Dear Jake,

You've worked in New York media for a long time. What would you advise a young person considering a career in that area? Good idea? Or look somewhere else?

Sincerely,
Would-be Writer

Dear WBW,

This is not a good time to join the world of media. It's not like the *Titanic* is docked and people are still getting on board. It's like the *Titanic* has already hit the iceberg, the ship is listing precariously to one side, and you want to know if this is a good time to join the cruise.

Every single area of media present in New York City is in the middle of a fierce disruption: television by services like Netflix, radio by Spotify and Pandora, and newspapers by the endless free information on the internet. Even web media is in crisis as ad rates drop, advertisers move almost all their business to Google and Facebook, and content supply continues going up and up. In short, there's no safe place to stand and, unless you enjoy reinventing yourself every three years, there are better industries in which to ply your trade.

Writing is a fairly transferable skill; you can use it to write reports for not-for-profits as easily as newspaper columns. Same goes for photography, design, and editing. Now, if you're a TV weather person, it might be more difficult; some jobs must be done in media or done nowhere at all. In that case, you must ask yourself "Knowing the difficulty of finding steady employment in this area, is it worth it to me to proceed, or should I hang up my weatherman suit and keep this as a fun hobby to practice in my spare time?"

I didn't actually make a deliberate choice to have a career in media. My friend Jen Chung and I were both working for dot-com companies, and when the crash happened in 2001, we found ourselves with a lot of spare time. We used that time to swap links we thought were interesting, and eventually I made a simple blog where our friends could comment. That became Gothamist, and pretty soon we had blogs in other cities, and I had to learn how to sell advertising to support them. I sort of fell into the whole thing ass-backward, and that was for the best, because as a conscious "Is this the right career for me?" decision, I might have been too practical or too scared to choose it.

Yes, it has been fun, creative, and personally fulfilling, but it is also constantly nerve-racking in terms of money almost every year. In any career where the supply of talent far outstrips the demand, there is ferocious competition, which can lead to a lot of gross behavior, like gossiping and smack-talking. I never liked that part of the industry, and pretty soon learned to avoid media parties and get-togethers. It was just too many people looking over your shoulder to see if there was someone more important in the room to talk to. Sounds like a blast, right?

Then there's the problem of burnout. You may love to write. But it is very possible, if you are forced to write on deadline day in and day out for years, that this thing you love may turn into a drag. It's kind of like sex—doing it once in a while feels great, but do it every day for money, and, well, after a while that's going to start to burn.

Then there is the problem of the media companies. The ones that aren't currently dying are under tremendous pressure to succeed. This means they have to set insane goals for their employees, whether that means the production of pageviews, blind fealty to Facebook's ever-changing whims, blockbuster book sales, or TV ratings. To say it's a pressure cooker would be a massive understatement. Plus, it's not like these media companies give you absolute freedom to write what you want; there's often an unspoken agenda at play that you will have to follow, whether you support it or not.

What type of agenda? Well, sometimes it is political—many newspapers, television stations, and radio channels are owned by conservative billionaires who use them to advance their political beliefs. Even here in New York, one of the country's most liberal cities, two out of the four daily newspapers follow a conservative line, and they will take just about any chance they get to slap down a liberal politician or political movement. This can be an obvious slant, such as always using the most unflattering picture of the politician they despise, or it can be a subtle thing manifesting in the stories they choose to highlight and the ones they choose to bury each day.

Even the media outlets owned by large corporations with no declared political ideology have one; it's the total dedication to making as much money as possible. This yields a constant stream of stories designed to excite your lust for materialism and celebrity. It explains the style and real-estate sections in every city newspaper and magazine. Reading this stuff is what the Buddhists refer to as "eating poison"—it might be good for the corporation's bottom line, but it encourages unquenchable desire in its readers. Do you really want to be involved with that kind of system?

True, there are still small pockets of antiestablishment spirit left—small alternative weekly newspapers, independent blogs, and underground zines. They exist to speak truth to power, and they often do it quite well, but they are working with the same economics that are felling their larger mainstream media competitors, and things aren't looking bright for the future right now. What we really need, and are beginning to transition to, is a reader-supported, not-for-profit media ecosystem where the pressure and corruption of advertising has been removed, and where journalism is valued as an indispensable democratic institution. If you do feel a die-hard interest to become involved with media, seek out those opportunities, or better yet, start a company like that yourself.

Don't suffer in vain,
Jake

Dear Jake,

I'm burning out at my job in tech. We work 9 A.M. to 7 P.M. or later most days, and sometimes I have to come in and do the same on weekends to hit project deadlines. The work is otherwise pretty good, and there are the standard tech perks, like free food and drink. But I just feel like I never get to see my friends, go to the gym, or just relax like a normal person. Yes, I do get paid well, but I have to ask, "Is there another way to live here in New York? Is it possible to have a work/life balance here?"

Yours truly,
Sick of Work

Dear SOW,

It's possible to find a work/life balance in New York, but it is difficult. You will have to slay two demons that are keeping you at a job that's making you sick: first, the need for money, and second, the need for status. Many people have internalized these beliefs from our crazy culture and malignant media, and they do not even realize they have them until they begin to crack up or burn out.

All jobs come with some level of work stress, but there are plenty in New York that offer more regular hours than the one you have. Think of working for the city or state in a unionized public service job. You might be surprised to learn the average base salary is about $65K; at some agencies, the average salary is over $100K. Then there are the benefits, which can be as much as 50 to 100 percent on top of the actual paycheck. There are also tenure protections—more than half of city employees have them, which is a great way to reduce the stress of never knowing when you might be fired.

You might say, "No, I could never live on that salary—it's way too low." Untrue: The median *household* income in New York is about $50,000, so plenty of people are making a go of it on much less. What about housing? Well, as we've discussed, you could get a roommate or move to a more distant neighborhood. Think about it: Would you trade a smaller apartment in a less-central place for having a balanced life? Surely the choice is clear. So why is it so hard to trade a life in the fast lane for something more fulfilling?

First, you've gotten used to it. After a while of earning big bucks at Google or Facebook, eating out a lot, and enjoying a sweet apartment in a nice neighborhood, you may be unwilling or unable to give up all of that stuff. Why not try an experiment and give up some of it for a week? Cook in instead of going out, don't buy anything on Amazon, and share a twelve-dollar bottle of wine at a friend's apartment instead of hitting the bars. You may find what you thought was so essential is actually quite easy to live without. You could also take a week off and just enjoy a slower life around the city to see if it suits you—actually go to the gym, walk in the parks, go to the museums—imagine what life would be like if you could do more of this.

Second, it may not just be the money that's holding you back. A lot of people derive their inward sense of self worth from high-status employment. This is the thing that gives you a little boost when someone asks what you do at a party. Going from a fancy job at a well-known company to working for the city or a smaller, lesser-known firm means giving up that status. But that is for the best—self worth built on job status is precarious indeed. You could get fired, and then where would you be? Better to give up the whole idea of status and focus on better values: living in the moment or helping others, for instance.

Third, the media bombards you with messages every day that make maintaining healthy values difficult. All those ads for new products subliminally convince you that if you just had that one new thing, you'd finally feel good. Of course, that requires more money. Or consider our television shows and movies and how often characters are de facto wealthy or well-off, or how they seem to effortlessly reside in homes three times the size of yours. In screenwriting, this is called "wish fulfillment," and it's an insidious, materialistic component built into most mainstream narrative entertainment (and advertising). All of it is designed to inflame your desires and keep you on the hedonic treadmill, lusting after one thing and then another, never satisfied, always suffering from a secret feeling of inadequacy that can seemingly only be remedied by more money and things. If you can, restrict your media intake to healthier sources: public radio and television, a few high-quality magazines. Avoid daily newspapers, especially the real-estate and style sections, which are filled to the brim with this venom.

Something else to contemplate: You may have to get some new friends. After all, most of your present posse probably embraces those same values of materialism and status and haven't yet had the spiritual awakening that you have had. They may not even feel like they're missing out on anything, working sixty or eighty hours a week in the rat race. They might also resent you if you switch to something that offers a better balance: After all, there's nothing more frustrating than seeing someone who had the courage to make a change like that when you're not yet able. You could try talking to some of your friends, explaining that you're burned out and there's more to life than work—maybe a few have been feeling the same way—but you also might want to build new friendships with individuals living a slower, healthier lifestyle. Where can you find such people? Yoga classes and coffee shops in the middle of the day seem like a good place to start.

Burnout is your body's way of telling you that you've got to make a change. Maybe you're not supposed to be sitting in a cube farm all day. Maybe your true destiny lies in teaching in a classroom or planting trees in parks. You'll never know until you start exploring your options and seeing what a slower-paced life could bring.

To a healthier future,
Jake

Dear Jake,

I know Jesus said "the poor will always be with you," but New York seems to have more poor people than most cities. This got me thinking, how do poor people survive in one of the most expensive cities on Earth? It's hard enough for me, clinging to the lower rungs of the middle-class ladder, but a lot of people I see on the subway look like they're doing worse. How do they manage to stay here?

Yours truly,
Not Poor, Not Rich

Dear NPNR,

I find it hard to believe that you can realistically spot poor people on the subway. Clothing and shoes have become much more affordable since trade was liberalized in the 1990s, and most of our garments started getting produced by sweatshop labor in developing countries. Long gone are the days when New York's teeming poor wore rags and dirty overcoats—today you'd have to look pretty closely at the labels to notice how expensively someone was dressed, and even then, our rich and poor wear many of the same affordable brands (Uniqlo, Forever 21, H&M, Zara, etc.). Even for the traditional luxury purveyors, like Yves Saint Laurent, Burberry, and Versace, thousands of convincing knockoffs are sold every day down on Canal Street.

That's not to say that New York doesn't have poor people; we always have: since the first slaves arrived in New Amsterdam in 1626, straight through the waves of immigration that continue today. More than 20 percent of our households live below the poverty line, and more than 30 percent are getting by on less than $20,000 per year. How can people live on such small incomes? The answer is cheap housing and cheap transportation. Both of these are dwindling resources.

As gentrification reaches further and further into the outer boroughs, rents climb ever higher. For generations, poor families got by here by subdividing tenement apartments in the poorest neighborhoods, but with rents climbing even in East New York and the South Bronx, this option is rapidly vanishing. At the same time, the federal government has cut back on housing vouchers that make up the difference between the market rent and what the poor can afford.

Then there's our rapidly disintegrating supply of public housing: 177,657 apartments housing 403,275 residents. Always underfunded, these public housing projects are falling apart, and without drastic and expensive repairs, they may not last to the end of this century. If current trends continue, we might be facing a city with the poor squeezed into small islands of remaining projects surrounded by a sea of expensive real estate. The remainder of the needy will either have to move to distant suburbs, new cities, or else become homeless, joining the 60,000-plus people already living in emergency housing in New York City.

Transportation isn't getting any cheaper, either. For generations, the poor got by using our city's affordable bus and subway system when fares were less than a dollar well in to the 1980s. Not so today: The impoverished often don't have the liquid savings required to buy monthly $121-MetroCards with their built-in discounts, and they end up having to purchase one-off swipes at a usurious $2.75 per trip. That's still cheaper than owning a car, but there could be a time in the near future when that classic image of rich and poor rubbing shoulders on the subway becomes a historical relic, as rising subway fares increasingly confine the underclass to their few remaining neighborhoods.

This matters—and not just because the city can't run without a reliable supply of workers willing to take minimum-wage jobs, particularly in industries like tourism, healthcare, and food service. The city's vitality depends on the mixing of rich and poor—think about the jazz age in Harlem, when the swells from downtown came up to see how the other half lived. Or the scenes in the most interesting neighborhoods over the last thirty years—SoHo during its cold-water artist-loft days, Williamsburg before gentrification sterilized it, or Bushwick today. In all of them, the energy comes from rich and poor interacting in close proximity and exchanging energy and ideas.

If New York isn't to become a monoculture of the rich and upper-middle class, we're going to have to act quickly. This will mean building more affordable housing and repairing the affordable housing we already have. It will mean making sure the impoverished can get to work by discounting subway fares that have soared beyond reach of the working poor. And it will mean a wholesale realization that our low-income families must be included in decisions that will affect them—about zoning, about schools, about access to hospitals.

You asked a good question. It is remarkable, in a city where the top 1 percent average more than two million dollars in income per year, how so many survive on so little. The next time you vote, or give to charity, think about ways you can make their lives a little easier.

Sincerely,
Jake

CHAPTER 8

How to Live Here Without Losing Your Shit

Questions

A hundred times I have thought: New York is a catastrophe, and fifty times: It is a beautiful catastrophe.

—LE CORBUSIER

Dear Jake,

Sometimes I need a break from the city. It's as if my brain gets too saturated with the noise and crowds, and I just want to go to a place where things are quiet and recharge. I could obviously take a vacation, but I'm looking for places I can integrate into my daily routine. Do you ever feel this way? Where would you go?

Sincerely,
Desperately Seeking Quiet

Dear DSQ,

Yes, of course I've felt this way! Could any New Yorker experience the constant stimulation of our great city without occasionally needing a break? This is especially true for introverts like me. I find dealing with lots of people to be exhausting, and I often feel the need to seek out a quiet place to chill. This can be a period as short as a fifteen-minute walk or as long as a full-day trip spent not talking to anyone, just absorbing the quiet and slowly feeling refreshed.

The most obvious place to go, of course, is a park. Central Park and Prospect Park have a number of less-popular areas where you can walk— the Ramble, the Ravine—often they're wooded and you feel like you've stepped out of the city into an enchanted forest. Sure, the enchantment is occasionally marred by people having public sex or homeless guys setting up camp, but for the most part, as long as you don't disturb them, they won't disturb you.

For an even quieter time, consider a trip to one of the more distant parks. The Jamaica Bay Wildlife Refuge is an easy trip on the A train, and you'll find that it's wonderfully quiet except for the sounds of the birds. Or head up to Bronx Park and visit the trails behind the New York Botanical Gardens; they provide miles of silent reflection. Or, if it's winter, consider a trip to the beach: Fort Tilden is incredibly still and fun to explore in the snow. Many New Yorkers also find peace there in the summer—swimming out to the sandbar and staring out at the horizon can be deeply restorative.

If you don't have time for a park visit, there are plenty of places where you can find a precious pocket of solitude. If you live in a quiet neighborhood, like I do, just taking a walk around at night is a great way to clear your head and prepare for the next day. Few people are out, except for dog walkers, and you feel like you have the whole city to yourself. If you're the brave type and live near the rivers, one of the most calming walks I like to take is along the river greenways at night. Brooklyn Bridge Park, East River Park, and Hudson Park all make excellent places to be alone, and there are enough after-dark runners and bikers to keep you feeling safe.

Counterintuitively, I've found that some crowded places are good for finding islands of stillness. For instance, at the Metropolitan Museum of Art, many areas, like the Asian Wing, can be nearly empty even during busy periods—check out Astor Court, a courtyard transported from seventeenth-century China complete with a koi pond and burbling fountain. Likewise, at the American Museum of Natural History, some collections, like the Eastern Woodland Indians on the third floor or the South American Peoples on the second floor, tend to be totally deserted. Every large museum in the city has rooms like these—they're fun to discover and use when you need a break.

What if you're out walking around and just suddenly feel overwhelmed and need a place to hide? Churches are often open for quiet contemplation or prayer, and in New York, you're never more than a few blocks from one. Sit in a quiet pew in the back and just bask in the silence. Our few remaining bookstores are also great for this; the Barnes & Noble at Union Square, to pick one example, has tons of empty aisles and the staff rarely hassles you if you just sit down and read. Local public libraries can also be oases of calm.

What if you're at work? Well, you could go out for a walk and take advantage of one of the suggestions above, but I have another idea: try the roof. In a lot of the old office towers in New York, the roof is left open so maintenance staff can get access to the water tanks and mechanicals, and they make wonderful places to find some alone time. Just be careful not to set off any alarms.

Finally, there's always the solace of a quiet night at home, preferably in the bath with a glass of wine or on the couch with a blanket pulled over your head. That'll do the trick for almost any quiet seeker, and I recommend you do it prophylactically—if you spend one or two nights at home alone relaxing, you might find your brain needs less quiet the rest of the time.

To solitude,
Jake

N.B.: For people who need quiet, but hate being alone, there are silent meditation and yoga classes available all over town.

Dear Jake,

I moved up here from Arizona back in April, and I've enjoyed New York so far. There's so much more to do here than in Tucson. But now it's December, and for the last few weeks I've been feeling down. Some of it, I'm pretty sure, is Seasonal Affective Disorder (SAD): I have to be out of the house at 6:45 A.M. to get to work by 7:30 A.M. (I'm a teacher and our day starts early). There's so much to do after the kids leave that I usually don't get out until past 5 P.M., and it's already dark by then. So, except for the half hour I get to run out to lunch, I basically live in darkness, and I think my body just isn't used to it. How do you locals survive winter here?

"Warm" regards,
Shivering in Sunnyside

———————————

Dear SIS,

Good for you for recognizing the source of your winter blues and trying to deal with it. Some transplants are miserable for many seasons before they figure out what a New York winter does to a person unaccustomed to the challenge. Before you do anything else, I want you to gather some supplies: a pair of long johns or thick leggings to wear under your pants at all times (sweatpants work well for guys with looser jeans and no vanity), a large bottle of vitamin D capsules, and one of those natural-light sunlamps. With these three items you'll be warm, your immune system will be up to the immense challenge it's about to face, and your brain will be fooled into thinking it's getting more daylight than it actually is. Voila, your SAD will disappear.

That doesn't mean you're not in for a bad time. New York winters are cruel and can last well into March, and your delicate hot-house-flower constitution is going to face many challenges it has never seen before.

The first time you step into what appeared, on the surface, to be an inch-deep puddle of slush, only to sink in right up to your knees, you will discover just how much you are willing to sacrifice to actualize your New York dream. Especially when you see the locals laughing at you; watching newbies fall into corner slush puddles is basically a winter pastime here.

Winter serves an important function in New York: thinning out the weaker members of the herd to increase the city's stock of tough, sturdy citizens. Every year, immigrants in the thousands arrive, and every year, winter sweeps half of them away on buses or planes for points west or south. The ones who remain mix their hardy blood with that of the natives already here, and the result is a population with antifreeze running through our veins.

While you're shivering in your apartment, wracked by the second Severe Acute Respiratory Syndrome–level flu you caught from touching a subway pole with your bare hands and then rubbing your eyes, your shivering only interrupted by occasional visits from Chinese food delivery people bearing soup, we locals will be outside enjoying ourselves, appreciating all the delights of winter in New York. Those include the empty seats at the restaurants and bars we can't get into the rest of the year, ice skating at the rinks in Central Park, and marveling at the holiday train show at the New York Botanical Garden in the Bronx. Hell, some of us will even join the surviving tourists to catch *The Nutcracker* at Lincoln Center or visit the Rockefeller Center Christmas Tree (ironically, of course). You might even see us eating a bag of those roasted chestnuts they sell on Fifth Avenue, even though they taste like coal covered in cigarette ash—it's just part of the winter tradition here.

So, if you want to stay here, what you need to do is force yourself to do as we do, no matter how much your brain is telling you to stay inside and hibernate. You need to build up your resistance. Try this: Instead of scurrying from home to work and back, take some detours. Put on two layers of socks, buy a fifth of Johnnie Walker or a mug of hot tea, and march your ass across the Brooklyn Bridge. Or take a festive gambol through the outdoor markets at Bryant Park and Union Square or spend an hour trudging slowly on line to see the holiday windows at Saks. On New Year's Eve, go freeze while you wait for the fireworks in Prospect Park to start at midnight, or participate in the annual New Year's Eve run in Central Park. Shiver with the millions in Times Square—even the most jaded native has done that at least once. If you want to get really extreme, join the Polar Bear Club's annual New Year's Day swim out at Coney Island. Afterward, you can go to one of the Brooklyn Banyas—those are Russian hot baths in Little Odessa, aka Brighton Beach.

Personally, I love winter here. In my youth, we'd eagerly anticipate the first snow and then steal metal garbage can lids to go sledding down Monument Hill in Prospect Park. That was followed by emptying Swiss Miss hot chocolate packets directly into our mouths—I still have fond memories of those freeze-dried marshmallows—no ten-dollar Jacques Torres hot cocoa for us back then. Then, there were the legendary snowball fights. Or, more accurately, throwing snowballs at passing cars and then running from the angry motorists who'd occasionally jump out and chase us down the block. Once we tired of cars, we'd throw the snowballs at each other, but "snowball" is actually a generous term for what was actually a three-inch sphere of black New York garbage ice surrounded by a one-inch layer of fresh snow. If you caught one of those in your face, you'd remember it for life.

This was back in the bad old days, and it's not like the badness took a break from December to March. No, we'd spend afternoons getting chased down icy streets by the local teenage muggers, weighed down by the thirty pounds of textbooks our teachers mandated we carry in our backpacks from sixth grade on. I remember slipping on the black ice and bouncing ass-over-elbows right into the sooty snowbanks. In my teens, I lost a few puffy North Face jackets this way. Oh, sweet memories of youth!

Returning to you: Yes, you're in for some real unpleasantness, but take the advice above and it won't be a season of misery. Remember: If you wanted an easy life of warm winters, you'd have stayed in Arizona. No, you came to New York City to test yourself, to deepen your resolve, to increase your grit—and surviving these freezing months is the only way you're going to get to that destination. Buck up!

Or, I don't know, think about all the poor bastards suffering from six months of ice storms coming off the lake in Chicago. That always cheers me up.

To warmer days ahead,
Jake

N.B.: Never, ever participate in SantaCon, that most insufferable of winter bacchanals. It's just thousands of frat bros day drinking until they throw up on passersby, and it's widely reviled by all real New Yorkers. The No Pants Subway Ride, usually in early January, is a moderately more acceptable event, but it is still premised on acting weird to freak out strangers, which is never a good idea in a city filled with as many crazy people as ours. Idiotarod, on the other hand, is a stellar wintertime expression of zany NYC creativity—check that one out.

Top Ten Ways to Maintain Your Sanity While Working a NYC Job

1   Unless it's pouring, always take a walk at lunch. Humans were made to get some sunlight every day, preferably in a park.

2   Move around. If you're not standing up every hour, your body will eventually begin to collapse.

3   If you work at a desk, shift positions frequently. You can build a simple standing desk from reams of paper and books and switch back and forth.

4   Get an office plant. If you take care of something, it distracts you from focusing too much on work's miseries.

5   Befriend your coworkers. They're probably weirdos, but making small talk for half an hour a day is good for the brain.

6   Celebrate at every occasion: birthdays, the end of projects, when someone gets hired or takes a new job—you'd be surprised how much unhappiness can be lightened with cookies, beer, or pizza.

7   Take all your vacation days. Many people don't, but you earned them, and they're critical for living a well-balanced life.

8   Likewise, when you're sick, stay home. Your coworkers will thank you for not getting them ill, and nearly every business in NYC is required to offer its workers at least one week of paid sick leave.

9   Know your rights. If you're really being treated like crap by your boss or a coworker, someone is often breaking the law.

10   Remember: As stressful, boring, or poorly paid as your work may be, you still get to do it in the greatest city on Earth. It's a small consolation but an important one.

Dear Jake,

I'm feeling burned out on New York. The constant hustle to make money, the noise and crowds, the horror show that is dating here. The thing is, I don't want to leave; I just want to get back that feeling of infinite possibility I had when I first moved here. Is there any way to do that, or should I just pack my bags?

Thanks for any advice,
So Burned

Dear SB,

Sounds like you're suffering from classic New York Overwhelmed Syndrome: that feeling that even natives get if they stay too long in town without taking a break. It causes you to lose sight of all the reasons you moved here—those seemingly infinite possibilities and the rush you used to get from them—and just see the worst of the place: the stinking garbage, relentless crowds, and the ferocious competition for everything. Luckily, a cure is simple! You just need to get out of town for a week or two, let your brain calm down, and return refreshed. If you can't afford to get out, I can suggest a few staycations that might cure you.

First, the classic getaways: renting a cabin in the Catskills, or the North Fork of Long Island, or one of the quieter towns on the Jersey Shore—Cape May, for instance. All are within a few hours' drive, reasonably affordable, and have enough to do that you won't be bored. Remember: Your goal here is recuperation—if you wanted excitement, you'd be headed to Paris. Try to treasure the quiet and the slowness. Take long walks, cook your own meals, watch the sunset, and go to bed early.

I guarantee that a week or two away will have you seeing New York from an entirely different perspective when you get back. Suddenly it will feel like it's brimming with options, and even the garbage smell will feel like the familiar scent of an old friend. I remember, as a kid, driving back from the bungalows my parents used to rent upstate in the summer, and that first sensation I got stepping out of the car when we arrived home. That feeling of excitement, of new things to see and do, of a city just waiting to be explored and discovered again. You'll experience something like that, too.

What if you can't get away from the city for financial or work reasons? You can still take a day off and head to one of our city's quiet destinations: The Rockaways and City Island both offer summer respites from the hustle and bustle of the city along with long strips of quiet beach. Or don't even go that far—pick a quiet neighborhood and Airbnb. Red Hook, for instance, would be a quiet but fun place to spend a couple of days.

While you're on vacation or staycation, you need to think about why you got burned out in the first place. Were you trying to do too much, going out every night to bars or restaurants? Were you working too hard or packing in hours that were wearing you out? How are the relationships in your life; are any of them draining or toxic?

It's also possible that you're not taking enough advantage of what NYC has to offer culturally. Are you caught in a rut of going to work, coming home, and watching Netflix on the weekends, with a dash of drinking-with-your-friends mixed in? In other words, are you living a life that could be lived in the suburbs and missing out on what makes NYC so exhilarating: the live music, the theater, the out-of-the-way restaurants, the art and museums, the weird performance parties? If you're not soaking up some of New York's unique cultural riches, you're likely missing the point of living here. Subscribe (and donate) to an essential NYC events newsletter, like NonsenseNYC, and do something cultural at least twice a month.

If you set aside time to meditate on the causes of your frustrations with New York, I think you'll find that a lot of burnout isn't caused by the city at all, but by the way you conduct yourself while you're here. Change those habits and you'll never burn out on NYC again.

Namaste,
Jake

Dear Jake,

Last month I was coming home from work in Midtown and the crowded Q train I was on stopped right at the end of the Manhattan Bridge near the DeKalb station. The conductor announced that it was just "train traffic ahead," but after ten minutes the air conditioning went off, and fifteen minutes after that the conductor came back on and said there was actually a Q train stalled at Atlantic, and we couldn't move until it was cleared.

By then, thirty minutes had passed, the car was about ninety degrees, and people were beginning to freak out. Several people were cursing, and not just the usual crazy types. Someone on the other side of the car fainted, and, right then, for the first time in my life, I had a full-scale panic attack—heart suddenly racing, imminent feeling of doom, and buckets of sweat. Just as I was about to pass out, though, the train started up. I managed to push my way through the crowd at the DeKalb station, get upstairs to Flatbush, and walk the two miles home.

Still, since then, I've been a mess. I've had at least three panic attacks on the train, whenever we've suddenly stopped, but I also have a general feeling of anxiety and depression following me around. Suddenly, the city just seems unbearable, and like I'm never going to be able to keep living here. Do you natives ever suffer from problems like this? How do you keep your shit together?

**Yours,
Feeling Trapped**

———————————

Dear FT,

You have my sympathy. Every New Yorker, transplant or native, periodically runs into a rough patch like this: a day when the city finally overwhelms your last mental defense and you find yourself shaking in the face of the urban onslaught. While it sucks hard to suffer, know that these moments are essential to building up your New York toughness.

Viewed the right way, they are a wonderful opportunity to grow, and they should be embraced as such.

It's usually the subway; that's where most people lose their shit. There's something about being trapped in a crowded tin can, seething with germy commuters, in a dark tunnel, with no sense of when you'll be allowed to escape, that evokes the animalistic fight or flight reflex, and with the opportunity to do neither, your brain freezes up and you freak out.

Of course, some people have the luxury of biking or walking to work, or the good luck of riding one of the few subway lines that isn't constantly delayed (pretty much only the three S line shuttles). That doesn't mean they will escape their inevitable New York breakdown. No, something else will eventually trigger it: say emptying out the last dollar of their savings account to make the extortionate rent on their tiny apartment the same day their horrible roommate announces that her boyfriend is moving in, or the line outside the bagel place suddenly going two blocks long for no apparent reason, or one of their friends posting their latest luxury-vacation selfie on whichever social-media network is currently causing the most jealousy and self-hatred. There's always something, someday, that's going to knock you on your ass.

This is particularly true if you're a member of one of our city's many oppressed groups. Minorities have to deal with all the same bullshit as everyone else, plus a whole range of additional triggers: getting hassled by the cops for the millionth time, for instance. Likewise, poor people being told to report to their minimum-wage job on Christmas Day, "Or else." Or women dealing with the constant and insidious sexual harassment that goes on inside all of our city's major industries and on the streets. It's a wonder that mental illness, though highly correlated with economic deprivation, isn't more prevalent in our poor neighborhoods and among these groups.

When it's your turn to suffer, and it will be your turn at some point, remember: This is a natural reaction for creatures descended from chimpanzees (that evolved over the course of millions of years to coexist happily in African woodlands and savannas, surrounded by a close group of chimp relatives), and who now find themselves tossed into an over-crowded city of 8 million strangers. Your brain is just not naturally set up to deal with the crowds, the noise, and the smells. Of course, the human mind is endlessly adaptable—we have figured out how to survive in all sorts of habitats, from the frozen Arctic to the burning Arabian Desert—but, there, they don't have to deal with a cup of coffee suddenly costing seven dollars and garbage trucks howling outside your bedroom window at 3 A.M. every other day. You have to step back a little and appreciate just how remarkable it is that you're standing here at all and haven't run for the hills or some Podunk city like Boston.

Many New Yorkers manage to take this already-stressful situation and make it worse by attempting to medicate away their anxiety with our city's plentiful river of alcohol and drugs, which can be had in any neighborhood just about twenty-four hours a day. Sometimes, the drinking and drugging doesn't even spring from the anxiety—it's actually the other way around. When the partying you used to do in your twenties suddenly takes a dark turn in your thirties, every drink and puff and line seems to hideously transform into a ravenous worry monster just about the time you decide to go to sleep. For some, it isn't even the obvious addictions—coping mechanisms are frighteningly varied and include overindulgence in everything from sex and gambling to online shopping and food. If you're in one of those holes, do like the old expression says and stop digging and get help. It'll make the rest of this advice easier to follow.

What you need to do to overcome city-induced anxiety and depression is straightforward: Find your place here. What I mean is that you've got to build up a protective cocoon where you can retreat to from time to time when things get too messed up. First, physically, by finding a neighborhood and an apartment you feel at peace in, which, in these times of $3,000 one-bedroom rents, is no easy task in itself. Once found, however, you must not retreat to this safe space alone. Critical to alleviating dark clouds is to fill your environment with good friends, nourishing home-cooked meals, and creative hobbies. You'd be surprised at how much darkness can be expelled by having a nice dinner at home with a friend followed by the creative hobby of your choice: knitting, chess, crossword puzzles, a musical instrument, reading a book, etc.

Once you have found a safe place to stand, there are other tactics to employ: exercise, of course—half of the really crazy people I know keep their demons at bay simply by running a few times a week around the park. Anything physical is good; if you're not the exercising kind, try a cheap massage—there's probably a clean, inexpensive place three blocks from where you live, and forty dollars for an hour's worth of bodywork is well worth the price in terms of its effect on your brain. It helps if, while doing this stuff, you avoid shitty friends, their shitty behavior, and their shitty social-media posts—all of Facebook, Twitter, and Instagram exist to fan the flames of jealousy and then monetize them. Delete these people from your life and these apps from your phone.

A final technique: Find a way to laugh at the absurdity of your situation. For instance, isn't it kind of funny that a street could smell this bad or be this loud or be filled with nothing except real-estate offices and still somehow continue to exist? Or, isn't it kind of amusing how your roommate, who seemed so normal a month ago when you found them on craigslist, could turn out to be the literal worst person in a city of millions? Any situation can be turned around like this, and *should* be turned around—you'll feel better once you develop the wry "nothing surprises me" vibe that all longtime New Yorkers have.

Sadly, sometimes all this advice may not work. You may find that nothing you do seems to help, and those anxiety attacks or the crushing sense of failure or general inability to get out of bed overwhelms you. Then, of course, it is time to take advantage of our city's surfeit of mental-health professionals—therapists, social workers, psychologists, psychiatrists—we have tens of thousands of each ready to receive you. Yes, this can be costly, and yes, it may take some work to find the type of therapy or medication that works for you, but can you really put a price on your happiness? Don't take it as a sign of weakness. Every single person you know in New York has, at one time or another, reached the end of their rope and found themselves in the waiting room of a mental-health professional. This is not the kind of thing that people brag about, but get to know someone well and they'll eventually tell you about the time they had a total breakdown in a Starbucks bathroom line, or wherever, and who or what helped them get back on their feet.

But back to the beginning here: Your panic attack was your brain's way of letting you know you needed to change some things in your life for the better. Take this opportunity and treasure it! Only through acceptance of your human frailty and through nurturing your resilience can you achieve true wisdom, or stay in New York for long. And let's face it: What's the alternative? Moving to Jersey? Whatever it is, it's much worse than just picking yourself up, dealing with this, and moving on with renewed strength.

To better times ahead,
Jake

N.B.: If cost is your primary objection to getting therapy or medication, good news: New York recently changed its laws to force insurance companies to treat and reimburse mental illness on the same basis as any other kind of illness. If you don't have health insurance, or can't afford the copayments, call 311—the city has added several no- or low-cost treatment initiatives.

N.B. 2: There may come a time in your life in NYC when you cross paths with someone in severe distress, be it a stranger who seems poised to jump onto the subway tracks or a friend who disappears into a dark place. Do not hesitate to take immediate action when you sense someone is in real danger of self-harm. Do not leave the person alone; remove any firearms, alcohol, drugs, or sharp objects that could be used in a suicide attempt; call the U.S. National Suicide Prevention Lifeline at 800-273-TALK (8255); take the person to an emergency room or seek help from a medical or mental-health professional.

CHAPTER 9

How to Make Friends, Find Love, and Settle Down

Questions

New York City is all about sex. People getting it, people trying to get it, people who can't get it. No wonder the city never sleeps. It's too busy trying to get laid.

—CARRIE BRADSHAW

Dear Jake,

I moved to the city a few years ago, and I love it! I have a reasonably well-paying job at an ad agency and a Crown Heights apartment with two great roommates that I somehow found on craigslist. Sometimes I just take long walks around the city and soak up all the scenery and people and think about how lucky I am to get to live here. I really only have one problem, which is: I can't find a girlfriend despite about a million Tinder dates. It's hard to believe that in a city of this size I can't find a good match, but every woman I meet seems to fall into one of three categories: unbelievably stuck up, desperate to settle down, or super weird. What am I doing wrong?

Sincerely,
Undateable in Brooklyn

———————————

Dear UIB,

Maybe the problem isn't with all of New York's many dateable women, but with you! If, after "a million" Tinder dates, you haven't found anyone you like and who likes you back, I'm guessing either that app is a waste of your precious time, or you've caught New York's most contagious sexually transmitted disease: having unrealistic standards for possible mates. This is a natural consequence of being new to the city and overwhelmed by all of the options on the menu. Everywhere you look there's a fresh opportunity—a new place to eat, a new job to get, a better neighborhood to live in. Ask yourself if it's possible you carry this mindset with you when you go out on a first date: Instead of trying to see the best in this new person, are you just finding flaws and looking for reasons to keep flipping through some list? This is a great way to stay single forever, always sure that some better, more perfect mate is going to come along. Abandon this delusion and you'll quickly find the city teeming with great matches.

If you had asked me this question back in the ancient past, say 2010, I would have told you that the best way to meet potential mates is to expand your opportunities by living a more interesting life. Instead of just schlepping straight home from work and back, or out to the bar with your same roommates or three friends, you should find some activities where you could meet different kinds of people. The classic example was the Williamsburg kickball league, which drew twenty-somethings from all over the city. Before and after the games, waiting around for your match to start, or at the bar with everyone afterward, dozens of relationships were sparked between people who would have never met otherwise.

The kickball and softball and bowling leagues continue, along with similar opportunities, like volunteering, local political activism, going out to trivia nights at bars in new neighborhoods, or attending your coworker's cousin's friend's roof party. There are so many ways of getting out of your bubble and meeting new people. Unfortunately, all of these require you to get off your ass and actually go someplace, whereas the internet dating apps let you just sit on your couch, or at your desk at work, swiping through a seemingly endless list of faces and throwing out hookup requests like confetti.

This spray-and-pray approach is great if what you want is a super-ficial fling or a one-night stand with a stranger, but it's a terrible way to cultivate lasting connections. That's because these apps encourage you to treat people as just one more consumable good to be ordered and then discarded. Where the old, in-person methods let you slowly get to know someone and ease into a possible date, Tinder and Hinge and Grindr, and all their copycats, rush the whole process. You're essentially going from strangers to a first date with nothing in between and no context at all, which is almost always a guarantee for an awkward meetup.

I can see how this has warped your brain, even in the short time you've been in New York. You're already classifying women into mental bins: too into herself, too into you, too into stuff that you don't understand and don't want to make any effort to understand. To have any hope, you must wipe this habit from your mind, and preferably delete those apps from your phone. Get back into the real world, meet some friends-of-friends, and try going on a few dates before you start passing final judgment on people.

You're probably too far gone with your Tinder addiction to do this, but you could at least try to show up for a date with an open mind. Instead of "What can this woman do for me," think "What can I do to make this night more fun for her?" You'll be amazed at how much more enjoyment you have when you get out of your own head and think about someone else for a change. It's quite liberating.

One thing that will help is to stop meeting people for first dates at bars or coffee houses. These are literally the worst places to meet someone for the first time, because 100 percent of their attention gets focused on you, and that kind of intensity is something best saved for future encounters. Instead, try to make use of New York's many, many other options for first-time meetings. Take a walk around Central Park, or go to MoMA and see an exhibit, or stroll along the High Line, or wander around the Brooklyn Flea market. Anything where you can still talk, but where you can talk about something other than yourselves. You won't feel as much pressure to decide whether you like this person and whether she likes you; instead, you can talk about safer subjects—what you love or hate about the city, where you like to go when you have free time, etc. After an hour or two, you'll know enough about her to judge whether it's worth having a more intense date at a bar or restaurant, and if not, no big deal; you've just had a nice outing enjoying the city.

In New York, where everything moves FAST FAST FAST, you need to slow things down. Sex on the first date is a bad idea if you want anything more meaningful than a one-night stand. Work up to that over a few weeks and use that time to get to know each other. While you do that, try to talk about yourself less and ask questions of your new friend more. I recommend the classics: What's your favorite place to eat in New York? What do you love or hate about your job? Do you see yourself living in New York forever? Lighter is better. If you find yourself talking about whether you want to have kids during the third date, you've gone way, way, way too far.

There is one factor, above all others, you need to consider during these early days: Where does this person live? As a new arrival to our city, this might not seem like a priority; after all, we've got a 24/7 subway system and plentiful taxis—who cares if you live in Crown Heights and she lives on the Upper West Side? Let me clue you in: For every additional subway stop between you, the chance of a long-term relationship working out goes down by about 5 percent. During the week, just squeezing in a date after the ten hours your boss requires of you is difficult, but squeezing in a date when you have to schlep halfway across the city is almost impossible. No potential mate is going to feel worth it if seeing her involves two hours on the subway. So stick, as much as possible, to partners who live in your borough, or better yet, within walking distance. Romance blossoms much more easily when hanging out takes less effort.

So, remember: branch out, slow down, lighten up, and find someone within a comfortable proximity. If you do these things, I guarantee you'll find yourself in a serious relationship in a month or two.

Have a good time!
Jake

Dear Jake,

I'm a native New Yorker. Most of my family goes back seven or eight generations to the Irish who came over during the potato famine around 1850, plus some Italians and Jews who mixed in a few decades later. Since then, many branches of the family moved to the suburbs and other states, but my side stayed. Since at least my great-grandparents, we've been living mostly in Bay Ridge, Brooklyn, and parts of Staten Island. I take my heritage seriously; I never wanted to leave and so I went to Brooklyn College and later got an apartment with friends in Sunset Park. That was five years ago now and I'm doing fine. Good job with the city, good friends, and a cheap apartment near the subway.

About a year ago I met a girl on Tinder. For the first few months we were just hooking up but since then we've gotten pretty serious. There's talk of me moving into her place, getting married, the whole nine yards. My problem is she's from Texas, and she's not 100 percent sure about wanting to live in New York for the rest of her life. Also, though she finds my family and old friends amusing, they haven't really accepted her and still make fun of her Southern accent and cluelessness about New York stuff, like calling the trains by their colors or mispronouncing literally ever Italian dish my mom has served.

My question comes down to this: Can natives marry transplants and really make it last?

Thanks,
Lifer from Brooklyn

Dear LFB,

Of course natives can marry new arrivals and have long and happy marriages. Look back through your own family tree and think about how each wave of immigrants intermarried with the next to the point where you have blood from every poor country in Europe coursing through your veins. More than a third of our neighbors were born in foreign countries, and that doesn't even include states like Texas, which are practically foreign countries. Add it all up and the dating pool is probably two-thirds transplants, and if you filtered all of them out, you'd be cutting off a lot of potential matches. What's more, it's not like dating another native is an instant match: You've probably got as much in common with people from the Upper East Side or Flushing as you do with people from New Mexico. So appreciate what you have. There may be other reasons not to keep this relationship going, but where she's from isn't one of them.

Note, also, that the most interesting people in New York City are the ones whose families span multiple cultures. There are West Indians in Crown Heights who ended up marrying Orthodox Jews (rare, but true!); Asian-Americans from Canal Street who ended up with Puerto Ricans from the Lower East Side; even some traditional enemies, like Indians and Pakistanis getting together in Jackson Heights or Richmond Hill. If New York isn't overtaken by the rising ocean, in a few hundred years, everyone here will have forebears from all over the Earth, and every resident will be celebrating so many holidays that there won't be time for any ethnic hatred, or even going to work. Some describe this as a melting pot wherein New York takes in every culture, melts them together, and creates a unique and vibrant society. But the more accurate metaphor is the tossed salad where the traditions and cultural flavors are maintained but scrambled in all sorts of new ways. Something like thirty thousand people live within a mile of your house—imagine the limitless possibilities!

There are, of course, other deal-breakers besides state or country of origin. In this city you can hook up with people of vastly different ages, interests, sex habits, etc. By the time humans are adults, most of these qualities are fully baked and unlikely to change. Sure, someone from Texas can eventually learn to speak like a New Yorker, but someone who is into S&M is probably not going to be amenable to a purely vanilla sex life, and you're going to have to decide if that's cool or not. Likewise, people with personality disorders—the sex addicts who can't stop cheating, the very vain, the abusive drama queens (and kings), the lecherous power addicts who can't refrain from harassing their subordinates at work—some people are bad news and will always be bad news. Luckily, these problems lurk close to the surface, so you won't go very long without noticing them, and noticing how they make you feel like shit. Listen to those feelings and run away as fast as you can.

Her alleged desire to relocate to another city is, however, a serious issue that should be fully aired before tying the knot. If you are committed to your roots in New York City, as you seem to be, you must convey that to her with absolute clarity. If that's a problem for either of you, then you may want to take some time apart to really consider your priorities. Or you could let it ride and count on her gradually falling more and more in love with the city as she spends more time here with you. It's risky, but if she knows where you stand from the get-go, this might be a chance you're willing to take.

Returning to the question at hand, anxieties about stuff like this are perfectly normal at this point in a relationship when you're moving from "just dating" to "MAYBE GETTING MARRIED!?" Your brain is the product of hundreds of thousands of years of evolution, and it wasn't so long ago on the evolutionary timeline that pretty much everyone had to marry a cousin within their group or clan. So, of course, dating someone from outside your own culture or borough is going to provoke some hard-wired worries, not just within your own brain but within the brains of your family and close friends.

Ignore these false alarm bells and move forward, always remembering how lucky you are to live in a city where these possibilities can be realized. You could be living in Amarillo, where you only get to date other people from Amarillo: Think about that and shudder whenever you have your doubts.

To love,
Jake

Ten Best Places to Stroll on a First Date

1 **BROOKLYN PROMENADE.** Hands down the best first-date walk in New York, especially at sunset and afterward when the Manhattan skyline lights up like a jewel box.

2 **BROOKLYN BRIDGE PARK.** A close second. You can walk along the water for more than a mile, and there are plenty of lawns and benches and beaches to visit and enjoy the view.

3 **GANTRY PLAZA STATE PARK.** The Long Island City equivalent of the Brooklyn Promenade, also best enjoyed at dusk as the sun sets behind the United Nations buildings across the river. As with Brooklyn Bridge Park, there's a NYC ferry dock here, so you can extend your stroll onto the East River if the mood is right.

4 **CENTRAL PARK.** From Fifty-ninth Street and Fifth Avenue up to Bethesda Fountain, across Bow Bridge and around the lake; there's a reason just about every romantic comedy filmed in NYC has a scene from this walk.

5 **THE HIGH LINE (ON A WEEKDAY WHEN IT'S NOT UTTERLY MOBBED):** From Thirty-fourth Street down to the Whitney. It's a beautiful, unique experience in any season, and afterward you can have a drink in the West Village (or the Meatpacking District if you enjoy a European tourist scene).

6 **CHINATOWN.** Start on East Broadway and make your way up to Doyers Hook. Have dinner at one of the classic Chinese restaurants or drinks at one of the many hipster bars that have recently popped up around there. (The rooftop bar at the Hotel 50 Bowery offers incredible views of downtown Manhattan.)

7 **GRAMERCY PARK.** Walk around the perimeter of the park, sadly closed to the public, and then up to marvel at the Flatiron Building and have dinner at one of the many restaurants around Madison Square Park—Shake Shack, or the open-air food kiosks that operate there during warmer months.

8 **GARDENS.** In spring, stroll through one of our city's many beautiful gardens—Wave Hill or the New York Botanical Garden in the Bronx, the Rose Garden in Central Park, the Brooklyn Botanic Garden in Crown Heights, or the lesser-known but very serene Snug Harbor Botanical Garden in Staten Island.

9 **CONEY ISLAND.** For the most classic NYC date of all time, walk down the Coney Island Boardwalk and ride on the Cyclone or Wonder Wheel and get dinner at Nathan's. There's a reason this has been a favorite for a hundred years.

10 **DOWN AROUND THE QUIET BRIDGES OF THE GOWANUS.** The smell has dramatically improved in the last ten years, the views are great, and there are many new bars and restaurants opening in the surrounding area.

Dear Jake,

I'm a freelance writer in Bushwick happily dating a bartender who lives in Greenpoint. We've been together almost a year, and we're thinking about moving in together. Our main reason is money: My rapacious, parasitical, scumbag landlord wants a 20 percent rent hike when my lease comes up for renewal next month, and my boyfriend's roommate is moving to Los Angeles around the same time. If we moved into a one-bedroom, we'd save about 25 percent on what we're paying now, combined, which could mean a lot to us—a vacation once in a while, being able to go out to eat more than once every three months, etc.

My main reservations are that we're not quite at that place where we're sure this is going to lead to marriage, and rushing it could mess things up. Or, worse, we'll just end up getting married even though we're not perfect together, just because finding a new place in NYC would take so much work.

What should we do?

Sincerely,
Still Living with Roommates at Thirty-One

———————————

Dear SLWRATO,

You should definitely move in together. Dating in New York for a year is like being married for ten years in the hinterlands; if you can still stand each other, you're probably a good match. You must abandon the pernicious idea of a "perfect partner"—no such thing exists, and you don't want to screw up a good relationship looking for some mirage. Moving in with someone you like is one of New York's greatest gifts; not just for the reduction in per capita rent, but also because it provides a healthy togetherness that will insulate you a little bit from the hard times here. Ultimately, of course, you must go with your gut. Moving in with someone who you've got serious reservations about is a recipe for disaster, but if you've just got some normal pre-habitation butterflies, I say plunge straight in.

This advice does not apply outside New York. If there's no rent savings to be had because housing is cheap, and no major urban stress that coupling is necessary to protect you from, the downsides of moving in might outweigh the benefits. These are the places where people wait a year before holding hands, and then actually get married before moving in together, which seems both unbearably slow and dangerously foolhardy at the same time. Why would you wait until after you've made a binding legal commitment that's hard to unwind to discover if your potential mate has any deal-breaking habits—a preference for never doing any housework and treating you like a maid, for instance? My point here is that your friends and family who live outside New York may not understand your decision, but their opinions are based on an entirely different courtship calculus and must be ignored at all costs.

Let's examine your first objection: That signing a lease together might place unnecessary pressure on a good relationship and lead to a breakup. This will not happen. After a year, your relationship has already faced and overcome many stresses that you may not even be aware of: the endless opportunities the city provides to hook up with other people, all the schlepping back and forth between your separate apartments, the very high standards of your insanely judgmental New York friends, and so on. Dealing with these stresses has naturally already led you to discuss the big questions: how you manage your finances, how much crap you choose to keep in your apartment, your career goals, whether and when you want to have kids. These things come up much sooner here than they would anywhere else simply because of the intensity and difficulty of dating in the city. You're still happy with each other? Feel lucky and move forward in peace.

Is it possible you'll break up while cohabitating? Yes, just as it's possible you'll break up while continuing to live apart. Either way, your relationship could disintegrate at any time for reasons that have nothing to do with your living situation. But after this much time together, why not jump in and give it a try? You came to New York with a sense of adventure, didn't you? If you two are not meant to be, wouldn't you prefer to go all in and find that out sooner rather than later? Breaking up while living together is horrible, but let's face it, breakups tend to be forced tours of hell no matter what. You'll get through it either way if it comes to that, trust me.

Your other reservation: What happens if you do move in together and aren't miserable, but it doesn't feel as great as you had hoped it would— but, rather than face facts and deal with breaking up, finding another apartment, putting down another three months of security deposit, hiring movers, and all the rest of it, you just kind of float along like a corpse rotting in the East River, swishing around interminably between Hunters Point and Hell Gate? This kind of thing is also easily avoided: Simply ask yourself, right now, whether you can see staying with this person forever, despite their human frailties and annoying habits. If the answer is yes, then you're going to be 100-percent able to work through all the aggravating small stuff that goes along with any serious relationship. Eventually, you'll realize that the best person is the one you're with right now: the person you were willing to move in with, the person you can see a future with. Any other hypothetical options are just unzen worry traps, and indulging in them only leads to unhappiness.

We haven't yet discussed the best part of moving in with someone in New York: how it provides a cure to the egocentrism that this city creates. It's a normal human reaction to be concerned with yourself in such a crowded, fast moving place—if you aren't looking out for you, who else will be? But this can easily cross the line into self-absorption and a constant comparison of your life to the lives of everyone else, and a continuous worry about whether you're doing well enough. Moving in with someone forces a kind of intimacy where you end up thinking about someone else as much as you think about yourself: how are they doing, what do they want, are they happy? These kinds of thoughts are a path toward wisdom, which will only deepen once you get married, have kids, and face a whole new set of benefits and sacrifices.

If you do move in together, remember, you still have to put in work to make the relationship work. It's not like just sharing a bedroom is going to lead to long-term happiness or marital bliss. Keep having sex, keep going on dates, put your phone away for a few hours each night after work, eat dinner together, have a glass of wine and a real talk. This behavior will naturally lead to good communication, and that will be important because small fights are inevitable.

Someone has to take out the garbage on a freezing winter night, or kill that mutant cockroach family squatting in the kitchen, or wash the seven days' worth of dishes that you both allowed to collect in the sink. Some couples, though they do love each other, can't deal with these little provocations and, though they stick together, every bump in the road leads to increasingly frequent outbursts of mutual contempt. Avoid that kind of bad behavior at all costs. There are eight million people in the city who don't give a shit if you live or die. Always remember that no matter how annoying your significant other can be, they do care about you and your continued existence. Probably.

Good luck; love is a wonderful thing!
Jake

N.B.: If you really have serious worries about living together, these can often be resolved by taking a test-drive at one of your apartments for a couple of weeks. Most bad habits manifest quickly. If neither of your apartments will work because of space constraints or roommates, consider Airbnbing for a week, or taking a challenging vacation together, like a long road trip; really any situation that puts you together 24/7 so you can see how you do.

CHAPTER 10

How to Stay Here with Kids

Questions

You've got to fight for what you want. You've got to hustle. You've got to climb. You just can't sit around thinking shit's going to fall in your lap. You learn that by just trying to find a fucking seat on the subway and the bus. I was riding the subway when I was 6 years old.

—SPIKE LEE

Dear Jake,

My husband and I are thinking about having a kid, but it feels really daunting. First, there's the money: Neither of our jobs offers much paid leave (I'm a teacher and he's a journalist at a local paper), so having a baby would require depleting our meager savings just to stay home for a few months. Not to mention the cost of childcare once I go back to work; that would just about eat my entire paycheck. Then there's the home itself: Our apartment is a small one-bedroom in Inwood, which is claustrophobic with just two of us. It'd be hard to even squeeze a crib into the place, and that's no exaggeration!

Finally, there's the state of the world, which seems to be getting darker by the day, even here in New York. By the time this child grows up, it feels like the city is probably going to be a smoking crater or at least a ghost town populated only by finance bros, bank outlets, and real estate sales offices. What should we do?

Sincerely,
Contemplating Parenthood Uptown

Dear CPU,

You should definitely have this baby. You clearly want to and are hesitating because of normal concerns that can easily be allayed. Think about all the billions of people in the world who have it much worse than you financially and who live in horrible, violent, oppressive societies, but who still manage to reproduce and have happy children. You can do this! Once you do, you'll discover that having kids, and especially having kids in New York City, will be one of the best decisions you've ever made—one that will deepen your character and reveal a whole side of the city that was previously invisible to you. Honestly, don't even bother reading the rest of this essay until you've spent some time today trying to get pregnant—it's that clear a choice.

Let's start with your existential anxiety about the future. The best way to get over that is to think of all the previous generations here in New York City who had it just as bad, or worse, than you do now. Think about the baby boomers who were being sent to Vietnam to be slaughtered, and then spent their whole early adulthood living with the constant threat of nuclear annihilation from the USSR. Or their parents who spent their twenties on bread lines during the Great Depression, and then got shipped off to a war where half a million of them wouldn't come home. Or their grandparents, who fled the pogroms and poverty of turn-of-the-century Europe and then were forced to live in squalid, crowded Lower East Side tenements for years. Our presence on the Earth is living proof that each of these generations did its bit to ensure the continuation of the human species under circumstances remarkably worse than the ones we are facing now.

Having a child is more than an act of simple endurance in the face of a messed-up world. It's a hopeful move, a belief that it's better to see your genes and values propagate into the next generation than to let them die out now. This is an important attitude to have, especially for us New Yorkers, who often serve as one of the last bastions of humanism during the frequent periods when the rest of the country lurches suddenly to the right. Think about it: For religious and social reasons, people in more conservative states do not have your qualms about starting a family; if we let these hangups prevent us from having kids, then it's their children, and their sometimes ignorant, racist beliefs, that will dominate the next generation. You don't want that! Instead of thinking of your potential child as being delivered into a cold, hostile world, think of him or her as someone who will hold up a torch against the darkness and help deliver this country from whatever horrible mess our generation leaves behind: environmental disaster, rampant inequality, and social media, for instance.

Let me tell you about my own experience. My wife and I had been together about eight years, four of those as a married couple, when we decided that we were bored of the whole twenty-something scene: going out to the latest bar or restaurant, partying with our friends, whiling away our endless free time just exploring the city and not thinking about the future. The time for all that good stuff, which we had once so enjoyed, felt over and done with, and so we did what everyone we knew did when they reached that stage of their lives: We got a cat, moved to Brooklyn, and started trying to have children. One thing we learned is that, sometimes, having kids takes awhile—and the help of IVF doctors—and the longer you wait the longer it can take, so there is no time like the present to get going. Long story short, after two years, we were able to have our first baby, and it was great. He was super cute and much more interesting than the cat.

Like you, we didn't have a ton of money, and our apartment was very small. It turns out that neither of those things is a big deal. You're going to be so busy during the first years keeping this child alive, fed, and clean, that you're really not going to have any time to spend money on anything else. All the material goods that a baby requires have become surprisingly affordable, thanks to Chinese imports and craigslist. Yes, it will be tight, especially if you don't have family who can help you out financially or by babysitting, but it is survivable, and this period only lasts for a few years. God bless our city, with its free public pre-K, which covers kids as young as three, and the many social programs we have that provide food, health insurance, and housing to truly needy families.

What about housing? That one's easy: Get a pressure wall! These are temporary walls that can be installed in any apartment without damaging it and losing your security deposit, and they can easily transform a studio into a one-bedroom apartment, or a one-bedroom into a two-bedroom. We even took it one step further: When we had our second kid, we divided the only bedroom in half with the pressure wall to create two small kids' rooms, and then we bought a fold-out couch and slept in the living room. This went on for a couple of years before we saved up enough money to get a bigger place much farther into Brooklyn. Yes, living in a space that small with so many humans wasn't perfect: Whenever one of us would catch a cold, pretty soon we would all have it because of the impossibility of avoiding each other's germs, but on the whole it worked out well and let us keep our budget for housing low, which is a tremendous help during those early years.

To be sure, there are some sound rationales for not having a baby. For instance, if you accidentally got pregnant at sixteen and can barely take care of yourself, let alone another human being; or if you're one of those people who only wants a child to distract you from your own misery; or one of the selfish and vain who see having kids as one more status symbol to be acquired on the road to some imaginary finish line of "adult" achievement; or if you're a person who just can't bring themselves to give up the laid-back life that you lose the instant you become a parent. Having kids is hard, and nearly all-consuming, and in the early years, it leaves little time for anything else besides work or sleep. Half the time you feel like you're not doing anything right. So it's not the kind of thing you want to do on a whim.

But that's not your situation. You've thought about this, and despite your doubts, you're ready. You will soon discover, just as the parents of the other 100,000-plus kids born in New York each year have, that this sacrifice is well worth it. Not just because you'll have someone to take care of you when you're old, or the opportunity to meet a lot of new people through the parenting scene (and probably make your first new friends since college), or getting to see all of our city's many great children's museums and destinations. No, the main benefit is that having a kid is that it is the ultimate tool to force you to become a kinder, wiser, less self-involved person—this growth is inevitable when you spend literally every waking moment thinking about someone else. It's not that having kids is the only way to this self-realization—you can probably get there through any selfless activity, like volunteering, activism, or a career that helps others, but having a kid is the best, fastest, and most straightforward way for most people.

So do it!

Much love and happiness to your family,
Jake

N.B.: Sadly, often after much trying, some people discover that they can't have children. If you ever find yourself in this position, consider adoption. Just in New York, at any one time, there are almost five thousand kids who need loving families. Adopting is a huge mitzvah and probably the most selfless act you can undertake in this all-too-broken world.

Top Ten Kids Destinations that NYC Adults Actually Love

1 **AMERICAN MUSEUM OF NATURAL HISTORY.** Easily the most fun place to spend a day with kids. After you see the classic dinosaur and blue whale rooms, wander into the lesser-seen halls on the second and third floors where you'll always encounter something new, weird, and educational.

2 **NEW YORK HALL OF SCIENCE.** They've got a miniature golf course and about 1,000 really fun, interactive science exhibits to play with.

3 **THE NATIONAL MUSEUM OF MATHEMATICS.** This small museum in the Flatiron District is a mind-blowing visual experience that can be visited many times.

4 **NEW YORK TRANSIT MUSEUM.** Everyone, young or old, should visit this place at least once to see the old subway cars parked on a secret platform.

5 **THE NEW YORK AQUARIUM ON CONEY ISLAND.** One of the best aquariums on the East Coast, newly rebuilt after Hurricane Sandy took out a good deal of the old complex in 2012.

6   **THE INTREPID.** Poking around an enormous retired aircraft carrier never gets old; they also have a nuclear submarine and a space shuttle on display.

7   **WALKING ACROSS THE BROOKLYN BRIDGE.** Every NYC school kid does this at least once with their class, but no matter how many times you do it, it's still amazing to walk through those arches.

8   **THE BRONX ZOO.** One of the best, most humane and educational zoos in the entire country. Try visiting in the cooler months to get the whole place to yourself.

9   **GOVERNORS ISLAND.** Recently transformed into a wonderful park with incredible views, there are plenty of playgrounds, zip lines, and other activities for people of any age to spend a whole day on.

10   **CITI FIELD.** The better of our two baseball stadiums. Kids and adults will enjoy the Mets games, many food options, and the 7-train ride, which takes you straight across the rooftops of Queens.

Dear Jake,

My wife and I live in Astoria in a one-bedroom with a very rambunctious toddler and a neurotic dog. It usually works fine because there's an alcove for the crib and the dog only likes to sleep under our bed, but it can feel crowded at times, especially if you ever want ten minutes to yourself. Last week we found out that we're expecting baby number two, so we've been talking about whether it's worth moving out of the city, maybe back to one of the suburbs where we grew up (Long Island for me, North Jersey for her).

We both had pretty happy childhoods, but we don't really look forward to spending the next twenty years commuting into the city for work. Plus, we'd miss our friends and our neighborhood. But the cost of a two-bedroom apartment anywhere near here (and near a decent school) is, like, a million dollars and rising quickly. For that much, we could buy an actual house in Merrick or Montclair.

What should we do? Stay and deal with the challenges here or cut and run?

Yours,
Thinking About Leaving Queens

Dear TALQ,

If you want to risk having boring, entitled, narrow-minded children, and are looking forward to acting as their chauffeur to every activity, playdate, and birthday party until they are well into high school, by all means feel free to start packing. Likewise, if you really want to spend a significant portion of the rest of your life on the LIRR or New Jersey Transit lines, can deal with seeing your city friends only once or twice a year, and have no qualms about the tremendous damage suburban living does to the environment, it might be a good idea for you to get out of here. Your departure will free up an apartment for a New York family who actually appreciates this city, and in these times of record housing shortages and unaffordable rent, the lifers need every place we can get.

Growing up in New York, even in these relatively peaceful times, produces tough, street-smart kids. They experience more economic and racial diversity in preschool than most suburban kids see in their whole lives. In a country that's soon to be majority minority, feeling comfortable around all sorts of people—rich and poor, black and white, new immigrant, and tenth-generation WASPs—will help kids develop an ingrained tolerance that will be a real advantage once they have to face the real world. Think about it: Just walking around the streets of Queens, your kids cross paths with dozens of cultures, hundreds of different ethnicities, and people who are both very rich and very poor. Experiencing the lives of others and, especially, the suffering of others in our homeless, panhandlers, and blank-eyed shuffling drug addicts, teaches them so much that is impossible to communicate in any other way.

There's more. Kids here experience not just a diversity of people but a diversity of situations. Neighborhoods that vary from inner city to nearly suburban, the pleasures and dangers of riding the subway as a tween, the street smarts that you can only develop from having your backpack stolen by the local tough kids a few times. By the time these children reach college, they're already hardened and self-possessed and can take care of themselves. This is important because, when kids first fly from the nest, there are all sorts of temptations and opportunities to fuck up: drugs and booze, for instance. City kids know all too well what overindulgence in those things can do because they've seen the heroin addicts in Tompkins Square Park and the drunks in Union Square. By the time they've graduated high school, they've had plenty of opportunity to get wild themselves on the streets of New York, and have already started to learn their limits. So, come freshman year at NYU, they won't be the ones overdosing during orientation—those are always the suburban kids who are so ecstatic to finally cut loose in the big city that they go overboard at the first opportunity.

And it's not just the children who suffer in the suburbs; the parents suffer too. Especially the parents who have experienced real city living and have gotten used to all the great things we have here: the world's best museums, real bagels, bodegas where you can buy just about anything at any time within five blocks of your house. You're going to miss this stuff once you're living in some barren suburban wasteland where the most interesting thing to do nearby is Bobby's Burger Palace at the Roosevelt Field Mall, or some such horror show. You probably think that's not going to be you, that you'll be one of the families that come back to the city every weekend to indulge in all the culture you're missing at home. This will not happen. After commuting an hour (or more!) each way to your job, the last thing on earth you're going to want to do is come back into the city on the weekend. No, you'll stay where you live, in that comfortable, gradually deadening suburban bubble, as the best years of your life pass you by.

Suburban living isn't just a curse for those who resign themselves to it; it's also terrible for everyone else, even those of us who stay in the cities. That's because suburban living is terrible on the environment. First, there's the significantly larger energy footprint that it takes to heat a free-standing house versus a city apartment. Then there's the transportation. Those two cars you're going to end up needing for even the most basic errands, like getting your kids to soccer practice or buying a quart of milk, consume far more energy per capita than getting around by subway and bus. At a time when the polar ice caps are melting, what kind of message does it send to your kids if you're living like this? Is the environment someone else's problem? The other pernicious costs of suburban living also get foisted onto the rest of us—like the rising inequality when people of means cloister themselves from the rest of society, or the draining of government resources from projects that benefit the poor and the many, like subways, to projects that benefit the rich and the few, like highways. An honest choice between city and suburb would take all of these things into account.

My guess is that you've already considered some of these angles and that's why you're hesitating to leave, but you still don't know how you can afford to stay. Luckily, that's something we natives can help with. First, make the most of your small living space—pressure walls really are a gift from God, but there are other tricks. For instance: finding a good public school. If your local one has problems, like low test scores, overcrowded classrooms, or a lack of extracurriculars, the moral thing to do is roll up your sleeves, join together with some of your neighbors, and help the place improve through fundraising and encouraging more parental involvement. You won't be alone: This is happening every day in schools all over the city.

But let's say you don't have the time or energy for any of that. There are other ways to get your kids a great public education. One is to simply rent an apartment in a coveted school zone for the year that your kid enters kindergarten. Once the little one has established residency, you can move to less expensive neighborhoods nearby—they can't be kicked out once they're in. This usually applies to siblings, as well, and is such a popular technique that if you walk by a popular elementary school in the morning, it seems like half the kids are arriving by Uber.

It's also worth noting that the whole idea that suburbs provide better housing for less money is at best only half true and at worst a total lie. Before you even consider moving, take a spreadsheet and calculate all of the ancillary costs of life in the suburbs: car payments, property taxes, home-improvement jobs, monthly train tickets, winter heating, etc. And don't forget to include the opportunity costs of all that time you're going to be spending commuting back and forth to your jobs in the city—that in itself is very valuable. Once you've really factored it all in, the true price of suburban living might be significantly higher than you first considered, and though it is true that you will have a somewhat larger space to live in, it's not a great deal at all.

If you do decide to stay, don't vacillate. Make the decision once and for all to spend the rest of your life in New York. Once you stop worrying every two minutes about life being better or cheaper or easier somewhere else, you'll find that New York becomes a markedly more enjoyable place. Remember: You and your family will experience more here in one year than you would in Jersey or Long Island in twenty. And, though it will sometimes be a pain, when your kids are adults themselves they will thank you for letting them become real New Yorkers.

To city living,
Jake

N.B.: You could also always compromise and live a somewhat suburban life inside NYC, like in Forest Hills, Ditmas Park, Riverdale, or most of Staten Island. There are many such places, and you'll still be able to take mass transit to work.

Dear Jake,

I live in Red Hook with my wife and two kids. It's a great neighborhood. We've got Fairway, IKEA, and a whole strip of bars and restaurants down on Van Brunt Street. My wife is an artist with studio space a few blocks from our apartment, and I can bike to work in downtown Brooklyn. Compared to the suburbs where we grew up, it's basically our ideal life, except for one thing: The local school we're zoned for isn't great. Academically, less than half the kids are passing the state tests. Also, we're middle class and white, like only 14 percent of the student body, so our kids would belong to a small minority and we're worried about them making friends and getting bullied. There's a private school nearby that gets good reviews; it is $25,000 per child per year, which would be very difficult for us, but we could probably make it work.

Still, we have other reservations: In this age of insane social inequality, is it wrong to put our kids in a school where almost none of our neighbors can afford to attend? What would you do?

Thanks for the advice,
A Very Nervous Parent

———————————

Dear AVNP,

I send my kids to a Brooklyn public school, and you should too. Private school is a bad idea for kids because it restricts their exposure to other races and classes and gives them the false impression that life is easier than it actually is. Private school is bad for parents because it vacuums up every dollar you have that could otherwise be saved or spent on meaningful experiences with your family. Private school is bad for our society because, as you wrote, it magnifies inequality by isolating the rich from the poor, even when they live just steps apart in the same neighborhood.

First, let's consider the effect on your kids. Private schools have smaller classes, more extracurricular activities, and a teaching staff very attuned to the wants and needs of the parents (lest they pull their kids out and take them and their money to a different school). This is a molly-coddling environment where every child is taught that they are special, that their needs will always be met, and that someone is looking out for them every moment of the day. This, to put it mildly, is not how American society works, either in general or, particularly, in the case of New York City. When children who have been raised like this finally meet the real world in all its terrible indifference, competition, and hardship, they wilt like hothouse flowers or shatter like delicate glass.

I've seen this firsthand. I went to Stuyvesant, one of the city's most intense math and science high schools, which you have to test into in eighth grade. The next year, when we started, there was a large cohort of kids from Brooklyn. Some, like my friends, were from the average public junior high schools, and some came from the borough's top private schools: St. Anne's, Berkeley Carroll, and Packer. Long story short, after the first year, all the public school kids were still there, but many of the private school kids had gone back whence they came. Why? Because Stuyvesant was a vicious shark tank of sharp-toothed, self-motivated kids with tons of grit. The public school kids were ready for that environment after years of experiencing large classes, endless multiple-choice tests, and little personal attention. The private school kids weren't and felt miserable and lost. Just imagine what would happen to these kids if they didn't experience the real world until they graduated from Yale—it'd be ten times worse.

Hustle, adaptability, and resilience—private school kids often lack these traits because they are treated as consumers and their parents as clients to be catered to. With very few exceptions (military academies, old-fashioned Catholic academies run by no-nonsense nuns, etc.), the primary mission of these schools is to make the child comfortable and happy. Hustle comes from the opposite experience: being treated as one more replaceable cog in the great public school machine, having to discover your own strengths in a curriculum that is, at best, indifferent to your interests, and feeling uncomfortable and sometimes ignored.

Adaptability comes from facing these situations over and over, in many different forms, and resilience from surviving and thriving despite these constant pressures over long periods of time. Go the public school route and, by the time your kids hit college or working life, they will be hardened and ready for success while their private school contemporaries will still be mired in self-indulgence and entitlement.

It's not just your kids who suffer. Let's talk about the effect of private schools on parents. The most obvious consequence is the tens of thousands of dollars you will be vaporizing each year on tuition, your commensurate need to earn that money through long hours at work, and the constant anxiety about what would happen if you hit any of those rough patches that everyone eventually experiences in their careers. Remember: It's not just the regular monthly payments—your kid is going to be rolling with the rich kids now, and you will soon be bombarded with additional spending requests, from the Latin class trip to Italy, to a new friend's ski vacation to Jackson Hole, to whatever preppy attire or uniforms you'll be pressured to pay for. Think of all the things you could do with that money and mental energy—spending more time with your kids instead of working late, taking nicer vacations without constantly worrying about the cost, actually giving to charity—instead of giving to a school whose primary mission is the education of overprivileged children.

Even if you manage to keep your kid from succumbing to the status-obsessed peer pressure, you'll still have to contend with the psychological effects of all this: It's been shown that even with the same amount of money, people are much more miserable being a poorer family in a rich neighborhood than a richer family in a poor neighborhood. Better to feel fortunate than envious and inadequate. Don't put yourself and your loved ones in that sad situation.

We haven't even discussed the deleterious effects private school has on our civic life. For our public schools to work, we need engaged parents with money to contribute to the PTA and children who are well-prepared for academic subjects. Poor families often don't have this kind of time or money because of their daily struggles just to make rent and put food on the table. Their kids bear the effects of being raised in that stressful environment and often need more help in the early years of school. If all the rich families pull out, your neighborhood is left with a school that is short on money and long on kids that need a lot of support, and this is a recipe for propagating inequality into the next generation and making it worse. If history is any guide, in the next few decades we're going to see the results of this de facto segregation—probably the biggest revolt against the upper class since the tsar was shot. Do you really want your kids to be on the wrong side of that fight?

Even if things don't escalate quite that far, the segregation that private schools contribute to certainly makes life worse for both the rich and the poor; the former by piling up unearned advantages on the side of an increasingly privileged class, and the latter simply by being ignored. Think about it: Sending your kids to the local public school and rolling up your sleeves alongside other committed parents in your community is probably the best opportunity you will ever have to make a more just world. And that's what you want, right? You moved to New York for its diversity and the excitement that comes when people of all different backgrounds come together in one place. Use this moment to confront your own prejudices and mix with people you've avoided mixing with so far. If you really wanted to wall yourself off, you'd have already decamped to the suburbs. You want your kids to be able to walk to school and to have playdates with their neighbors rather than be bussed four neighborhoods over every day. Listen to those feelings!

So I urge you to explore the local option. Do not judge a school purely on its test scores or racial makeup. Actually take a tour. Talk to the other parents who have already taken the plunge—you may find that the school is actually a diamond in the rough. And remember, even if it's not perfect, your kids will still be fine. Most real education takes place at home as you read to them every night and model other intellectual skills for them to follow. If there are any gaps, you can use the money that you're saving on private school tuition to pay for enrichment activities after school: tutors, sports teams, chess club, whatever. Trust me, as the product of thirteen years of this system, it works, and you and your family will be better off for making the right choice.

Good luck!
Jake

N.B.: There are some cases where private school *is* justified, like if a child has a disability that requires services not available at a public school, for instance.

N.B. 2: If, upon sober, serious reflection, you just can't bring yourself to put your kid in the local public school, at least consider the other public options: There are magnet schools that draw in smart children from all over the city; charter schools, which are nominally private but paid for with public funds and usually provide entrance by lottery; and public schools in adjacent neighborhoods that you can sneak into using the residency trick (see page 223).

Dear Jake,

Our sixth-grader is going to a junior high school three subway stops from where we live in Windsor Terrace. Some of his friends are going to be taking the F train there and back each day, but I have serious concerns about our kid riding the subway without adults—he's small for his age. There is also the option of putting him on a school bus, but this is more expensive, and he really wants to go with his buddies.

What should we do? At what age should kids be allowed to ride the subway alone?

Sincerely,
Helicopter Parent

––––––––––

Dear HP,

You should let him go with his friends. There is security in traveling with a crowd, and it's unlikely that a whole group of kids will be kidnapped, mugged, or find themselves lost at the F terminus on Coney Island. Even back in the bad old days, when you couldn't ride one stop without some goons attempting to relieve you of your bus pass, it was normal for kids to use the subway by themselves starting in junior high. So, these days, when crime is at an all-time low and the greatest dangers on the train are manspreading and hogging the pole, your boy should be totally fine.

A kid's first independent subway ride is an important step on the road to adulthood. I still remember mine and even now can relive the frisson of excitement that came with it: A few friends and I took the F from Park Slope into the Village and walked down St. Marks and Broadway to Canal Street to visit the late, great Pearl Paint, where we bought some markers to decorate our denim jackets (this was the late 1980s). At that age, as it was for most kids who grew up in the outer boroughs, Manhattan was a mystery to me. I certainly had no idea how to get around the Village or where any of the big landmarks, like Washington Square

Park or Union Square, were on the map. So, of course, we got lost, and that was kind of scary (we had no cell phones to rely on, obviously), but I remember, after wandering around somewhere over by the Bowery and eventually finding our way back to the F at Broadway-Lafayette Street, a sense of real self-sufficiency and freedom that I didn't feel again until I got my driver's license at age twenty-two.

It is a mistake to deprive kids of these experiences or delay them until they get to high school. A life with no threats is no kind of life at all, and kids who grow up swaddled by overprotective parents usually develop a subconscious feeling of weakness and dependency, which naturally leads to anxiety later on. Being allowed to take small, calculated risks, like going out of school for lunch in third grade, walking to and from school alone in fifth grade, and staying out late in tenth grade—these are all important developmental steps in the life of New York kids. So, once in a while, they get lost, or are hassled by the bigger kids, or drink 40s until they hurl. How else are they going to figure out their way around, or learn when it is a good time to start running away or how to avoid drinking too much? Someday these street smarts could save their lives, or at least make them seem really worldly and cool to their college friends from the suburbs.

I'm practicing this with my own kids. We've had a big subway map up since the first one was born, and by age five he could tell you the exact transfers to get to Times Square or the Bronx Zoo. When all the other parents on the playground are trailing two feet behind their kids to make sure they don't fall off of anything, apart from the occasional glance to make sure they haven't wandered off, I'm usually reading the news on my phone or staring off into space. If they need my help, the kids ask for it, and if they get into a tiff with some other younglings, they work it out for themselves. I don't help with their homework, except to tell them to go and do it, and I let them pick their own activities and adventures on the weekends.

Sure, I'm not sending an eight-year-old up to the Museum of Natural History by himself, but once we get there I let him lead me to whatever he wants to see, not the other way around. So far, this is going well. I can't bequeath the NYC toughness that all kids developed thirty years ago but, at least compared to their peers, my offspring should be strong and self-possessed.

I think these are going to be important qualities in the future as the pace of change in our society accelerates and the chances of some abrupt break—like a revolution inspired by our tremendous inequality, or mass migrations sparked by climate change, or the replacement of nearly all jobs by robots and artificial intelligence algorithms—increase. I want my kids to be self-reliant and ready to deal with change. I'd trade 10 percent more hustle and grit for whatever meaningless skills gets kids into the Ivy Leagues these days—playing the violin or being a chess grandmaster. None of those things are going to help when the shit hits the fan—but being adaptable and tough always serves a person well in times of chaos.

Of course, you can go too far with this. I've known plenty of latchkey kids who felt neglected by their parents, and more than a few families who set no limits at all—smoke all the weed you want, Jordan, just pack another bowl for your *cool dad*. Those kids usually went off the rails and into rehab or Hare Krishna cults soon after they left home at age eighteen. Kids need parents who are present in their lives, help them avoid the big mistakes, and set a model for how to behave as an adult. But this doesn't mean rushing in at the first sign of danger—quite the opposite. When you feel that urge, look deep within yourself and ask, why am I doing this? Is it really to keep the kid safe, or is it about my own anxiety? Some parents just can't bear seeing the child they love in any discomfort at all. Others feel worried that if they don't help their kid constantly, they'll be at a great disadvantage in the achievement wars that seem to define middle-class society these days. Either way, deal with your own problems—don't act them out through your kids.

I understand that none of this is easy. New York, with its crowds and pressure and money, can be overwhelming for adults, and there's this natural urge to shield children from it for as long as you can. So I know it will take some energy to resist and let your kid off the leash, but it's essential for their long-term survival and happiness. Make the effort to unclench, celebrate the adventures and the fuckups, the bad breaks, and failures that sometimes come with them.

Let your kid fly free!
Jake

N.B.: Age twelve also happens to be the time when you can no longer sneak kids onto the subway without paying. The official rule is kids have to pay once they're over forty-four inches tall, which would be around age eight or nine, but all real New Yorkers let their kids duck the turnstyle until they hit puberty.

CHAPTER 11

How to Stay in New York Forever

Questions

You haven't lived until you died in New York.

—ALEXANDER WOOLLCOTT

Dear Jake,

I moved to New York after college, and I've lived here for ten years—through a variety of jobs, girlfriends, and apartments—but now I'm thinking of going home. Most of my family and old friends still live in and around St. Louis and, with all my New York friends settling down and having kids, I probably have more people to hang out with there than I do here. Plus, I'm just tired: from the latest huge rent increase from my landlord; from the endless grind of long hours at work, driven by the constant worry about being replaced by younger, hungrier, cheaper workers; from the very real threat of terrorist attacks—the latest one was literally around the corner from my office; and yeah, this might sound petty, but my favorite local dive bar closed last month and appears to be getting replaced by a Chipotle.

So a lot of things are making me want to leave, but I can't help but feel like shipping out is a defeat, like the city finally beat me and I'm running away with my tail between my legs. Is there some point at which a person can say, "I did fine in New York; I survived, and I left on my own terms"?

Please advise,
So Over It in Greenpoint

———————————

Dear SOIIG,

I hate to add to your misery, but there is no way to leave New York and somehow still claim victory over it. That prize is reserved to those who stay through all the good times, and particularly through the bad times like the ones you're having now. Leaving, even for superficially good reasons—getting into Harvard, a great job offer out west, or winning the lottery and traveling the world—is still leaving, and the awards New York gives for realness are only given out at the end. If you split before you die, you miss out on them. You can still claim to have managed life here for a time but, ultimately, either the city broke your spirit or you didn't want to stay badly enough. Either way, you left defeated.

This doesn't have to be your fate! The local rule of thumb is that if you survive in New York for ten years, as you already have, you can probably survive here forever. Most people have their spirits broken after just one or two years and run home soon thereafter. But a decade here shows you've already surmounted a long list of problems: finding housing, work, and friends—all the necessary components for a long, healthy New York life. What you're facing now is just the inevitable existential crisis that all transplants face: Do you commit wholeheartedly to life in the city, despite its pain and hardship, or decide that you never fully belonged here and have to go? Let's weigh some pros and cons before you get on that plane.

First, let's get into the right frame of mind by recognizing what a luxury it is to even have a choice. Most people on Earth spend their whole lives just five or ten miles from where they grew up, and they'll never have the money or summon the will to leave their hometown. You belong to a tiny minority who have this chance, and you already took it once when you moved to New York. Compared to a person your age living in Afghanistan or Sudan, you live a life of unimaginable freedom, and no matter what you decide to do next, you're still going to bask in relative luxury of almost certainly never having to face starvation or homelessness or war. Keep that in mind, and your own situation won't feel that grave.

Now, let's look at all the positives of staying in the city: everything you already have and love. I'm not just talking about the big-ticket stuff, like our twenty-four-hour subway, the most vibrant cultural scene of any metropolis in the world, all the best hospitals should you ever get sick, and whole universes of ethnic food and culture you haven't yet experienced. No, I want you think about the smaller stuff: your local bodega and its cat, your favorite bench under the weeping willow in that nearby community garden, all the familiar faces of your neighborhood when you're just out on a Sunday walking around. Over the years, I have spoken to many people who left and, sure, they do miss the Metropolitan Museum and the dim sum places in Chinatown, but the real regret comes when they talk about their neighborhood; that sense of closeness and community that we have here just doesn't exist anywhere else. Why live a life of regret?

Your problems sure seem like the beginning of a normal, post-twenties identity crisis that has very little to do with the city and very much to do with whatever deeper issues are getting you down. Maybe it's a problem in your love life—relationships that never seem to work out, or one that did work out but has now soured, or not getting into relationships in the first place. Or maybe it's not the people in your life but the natural fear of getting older and eventually dying—that one stalks everyone from time to time. You've made a whole list of reasons to leave—the things you're running away from. Try turning that around and ask what you're running *toward*. Until you figure that out, it's useless to move, as your angst will just follow you wherever you go. So put some of those moving funds toward a therapist and give it another six months. You still might decide to leave, but at least you'll understand why you're actually doing it.

During that time, you might want to contemplate the actualities of moving back to the Midwest. Sure, rents are lower there, but so are salaries, and then there's the cost of buying and insuring a car and heating oil for those long, frigid winters. Net it out and you might find that you're not saving a whole lot of money. Also, while it might be easier to get a particular job when there aren't two hundred people applying for it, your total pool of employment options will be much shallower. There are plenty of occupations here that simply do not exist anywhere else—rainbow-bagel baker, rainbow-bagel blogger—and quite a few industries, like finance and media, that have a much smaller presence in other cities.

Along the same lines, your worry about terrorism is equally incomplete. Yes, New York will continue to be hit by the occasional attack—

that's the price, for now, of being the highest-profile city in the country. But our total number of homicides continues to decline, and it's safer to live here than in nearly any other big city in the country. Last I checked the FBI statistics, St. Louis had about three times more violent crime than NYC! Consider all the faces of death peculiar to the Midwest: accidentally getting shot by a deer hunter or by a toddler playing with those plentiful Midwestern guns, or all of the ice-induced car accidents, bear maulings, seemingly dozens of active serial killers, frequent meth lab explosions, etc. When you add it all up, you're much, much safer staying put in Greenpoint.

I could go on, but I think you get my point: Your problem is one of perspective. Rather than considering the twenty other options you have for drinking when your local dive goes out of business, you focus on the loss. This is a sign of an unhealthy attachment to the past and an unwillingness to change as you get older. Think of the words of Norman Mailer, a particularly wise New Yorker: "There was that law of life, so cruel and so just, that one must grow or else pay more for remaining the same." You're paying with sadness and regret, and if you don't fix it, this outlook will continue to torture you wherever you live.

I've said what I can. If you still want to pack your bags, go ahead. In some ways, it's a good deed; New York is already packed to the gills, and your leaving will open up some space for a new immigrant who will appreciate living here more than you do. Don't feel ashamed, either. Literally tens of thousands of people leave New York every year and are immediately replaced by fresh blood. Their arrival brings new culture and new attitudes, and in general, replenishes New York's urban vitality. The worst thing you can do for yourself is dither, becoming one of those people with one foot in and one foot out, constantly thinking of moving but never actually doing it. This is torture for you and your friends who have to listen to all of your complaints.

Finally: Some suffering is inevitable no matter where you live, so never fall into the trap of expecting perpetual bliss or constant happiness. Rather, strive for equanimity, which, at least to us natives, is the state of not wanting to be any place other than where we are right now.

Cheer up,
Jake

N.B.: You could also try staying in New York but moving to a different neighborhood. Long Island City is just across the Pulaski Bridge from Greenpoint, but it somehow feels like a world away. Maybe you'll find a better fit there, just around the corner, and at least you won't spend so much on moving trucks!

Dear Jake,

It's January and New York is, like, ten below zero, and the only thing deader than the streets outside my apartment is my personal life: no real job to speak of (just waitressing and barely scraping by), no boy-friend, and generally no real reason to get out of bed, except to reset the internet router or steal food from my roommates. One of them recently left to take some great TV-writer job in Los Angeles. She's been incessantly Instragramming her allegedly fabulous new life for the last two months; it's all palm trees, beach sunsets, and chai açai bowls. Anyway, she's got an extra room and invited me out to stay. I'd have to kick in some cash, but it'd only be about half of what my rent is here, and she could probably hook me up with some writing work.

It's so cold and depressing here; why shouldn't I seek a new life in Los Angeles?

Yours,
Hating It Here

––––––––––––––

Dear HIH,

At some point, all New Yorkers are tempted by the idea of life in Los Angeles, usually at times when New York is at its worst: freezing cold, lonely, and overwhelming. Suddenly, maybe in a movie, or more likely in some acquaintance's social-media feed, you are presented with a near-opposite kind of life, one that seems to solve all the problems that have been getting you down. Perfect weather all year round instead of New York's messy and extreme seasons; cheap, beautiful bungalows with vegetable gardens instead of whatever rat-hole-size tenement bedroom you happen to be occupying; a laid-back life of easy jobs and plentiful free time to hike or surf or just sit in cafes drinking lattes instead of the miserable, competitive grind of work in NYC.

I get it. But I've spent many months in Los Angeles over the last twenty years—running *LAist*, the city blog, and staying with my wife's family on the Westside, and I can tell you that your idea of life there is an insidious illusion that will evaporate after three weeks, leaving you just as miserable as you are here, but in entirely new ways.

It is interesting that Los Angeles features in 95 percent of New York escapist fantasies. The reason is that almost all other large American cities are built on the New York model—high rises downtown surrounded by a ring of urban neighborhoods, which are surrounded by suburbs and exurbs and eventually farmland. New York perfected this model, so any other city similarly constituted, like Chicago, Boston, Philadelphia, or San Francisco, will seem a pale imitation to anyone who has lived here.

Yes, those cities do have their own semi-interesting geographies, ethnic neighborhoods, and cultural scenes, and I might be a little biased, but New York is greater in almost every dimension. Take anything that makes these places famous, like the skyscrapers of Chicago. Sure, they've got a few nice-looking buildings, but if you had to choose a skyline to stare at for the rest of your life, is it really any contest? Similarly, we've got better universities than Boston, better bridges than San Francisco, and tastier beef-based sandwiches than Philadelphia (who in their right mind would choose a cheesesteak over a pastrami sandwich?). Why fantasize about moving to a city that's similar but slightly worse?

Los Angeles is different. First, simply in its extent. Instead of compact, it is sprawling; instead of being easily navigated by mass transit, it requires endless hours in a car. (Almost six million people use the New York subways each day—the equivalent figure for the Los Angeles Metro is about 350,000. Although LA is investing in new subway lines, it will still be years before it reaches the ubiquity of our current system.) Ethnically, it has far more to do with Mexico or Asia than it does with the rest of the United States, which even I can admit gives it certain culinary advantages—their taco trucks and Korean BBQ places are superior, but are they so vastly superior to make up for Tinseltown's other myriad deficiencies? No way, LA.

And then there is the weather, which is temperate year-round, and all the things that weather makes possible: hiking in the hills almost any day of the year, fresher fruits and vegetables than any city east of the Mississippi ever sees, eating lunch outside in February, etc. It is this oppositeness that draws the mind of the New Yorker in, first in pictures and then for a weeklong vacation, and suddenly you're browsing for bungalows in Venice or Silver Lake.

Do not be deceived. First, you will discover that you will not be living in a cute little house five blocks from the beach. All of that real estate—from Venice to Santa Monica and east through the city through Hollywood, Los Feliz, Silverlake, and Echo Park—has been gentrified going on ten years. The only way that you're getting the cheap house of your dreams is to build a time machine or pony up more money than you're paying in New York.

No, you'll be living in one of those no-man's lands halfway to Pasadena or in the outer rim of Culver City. And instead of a Craftsman cabin, imagine more of a 1970s concrete box on stilts. Which is probably a good time to remind you that most of Los Angeles's buildings have not been retrofitted against earthquakes, and the whole region is about a decade overdue for the "Big One." Maybe you won't be kept awake by your neighbors screaming through the walls, as in New York, but try putting nightmares of getting pancaked while you sleep out of your head—that's much, much worse. I won't even get into the fires and mudslides, which are likely consuming about a quarter of the city right now.

The urban sprawl inevitably results in more hours trapped in your car, hours that will be unpleasantly spent in bumper-to-bumper traffic on the 10 or 405 or 101 or whatever freeway takes you to and from work. This unpleasantness is generally hidden from tourists who stick to hotels and Airbnbs in the more convenient neighborhoods and move about outside of rush hours. To get a taste of it, try driving from Santa Monica to the Arts District downtown at 5 P.M. on a weekday and explore the emotions it elicits from you.

This has a corollary when it comes to friendship, which is that you will never, ever, see your friends if they live on the opposite side of the city. In the rare event you have close friends who will even consider making the effort, you will spend hours negotiating where to meet. In New York, seeing your friends is easy, even if they live in different boroughs; you can just meet in Manhattan after work, get loaded, and take the subway home. This kind of thing simply doesn't exist with any regularity in Los Angeles because the distances and costs are too great. Even now, when the advent of Uber has made it possible to have more than two drinks and not get busted for a DUI on the way home, Los Angeles socializing is still light years behind New York's.

So you will schlep back and forth to work and generally stay close to home the rest of the time. For most Los Angelinos, even that requires a car, as only a handful of neighborhoods are walkable, and even fewer have enough bike lanes to make commuting on two wheels something less than a suicide mission. This is a city where most residents drive to the grocery store, to the bank, to the movies—all of the places you can get to on foot in New York. This means that to stay in equivalent physical shape, LA residents must make a concerted effort to exercise. Some of this can be enjoyable—hiking is a religion there, and on the popular routes, like Runyon Canyon, you see hundreds of people running up the steep slopes—but you still have to squeeze it into your schedule in a way that we don't in New York.

Likewise, the city is periodically swept by cultish fitness crazes—CrossFit being the most recent—and, at certain outdoor public staircases, you will witness people actually lining up to trot up and down, over and over. All this work, and the average person in Los Angeles is probably still less fit than the average New Yorker who gets all the exercise he needs just by walking around. There's an old saying about life in the two cities: That you should live in New York, but leave before you become hard, and live in California, but leave before you become soft. Speaking physically, this is bullshit: Humans are much better off being in shape than turning to jelly.

Finally, there are the people of Los Angeles, your prospective future neighbors. Many, of course, are normal working people who live their lives, do their jobs, spend time with their families, and generally don't bother anyone else. These, for many reasons, are not the people you will be hanging out with. No, being a new arrival generally means getting thrown in with the other rootless young metropolitans. Most of these people have been drawn to Los Angeles to work in some area of the entertainment industry, which still dominates the city like a colossus. At cafés, markets, parks, gyms, museums, and beaches, you will hear them talking, endlessly, about their unproduced scripts and uncasted parts, about studios, grosses, agents, TV deals, on and on. It's possible that this stuff interests you, professionally, but after awhile you will reach your limit and long, wistfully, for the diversity of New York City, where a stranger at a party could at least be a banker or a journalist or something.

The industry brings along with it an economic inequality that's far worse than what you find in New York. Yes, we, of course, have the Upper East Side right next to East Harlem, but people from both of those neighborhoods have to wait together on crowded 6-train platforms. Not so in Los Angeles, where the residents of Bel Air, or Beverly Hills, or Pacific Palisades, can spend a lifetime interacting with almost no poor people (with the exception, of course, of their maids and gardeners). At most, in Los Angeles, the rich share a freeway lane with the poor, seldom glancing out the windows of their $150,000 Teslas to notice a beat-up pickup truck full of leaf-blowers as it slowly passes by.

This inequality has malignant effects. For one, it encourages many of the richer areas to secede and form their own pockets of heavily insulated prosperity, while poorer people are left to make do with what's left in a sprawling and underfunded county. Yes, New York also has the poorly performing schools this kind of urban balkanization produces, but all neighborhoods receive the same trash collection, sewer maintenance, and road resurfacing. Not so in LA—you can actually feel the inequality as you drive. Some stretches, even of fancy streets like Wilshire

Boulevard, get considerably bumpier when you pass out of the islands of wealth and into the rest of the city.

I could go on about the Santa Ana winds and the strange mood of unease they produce for weeks each winter; or about the air pollution that can set in for days at a time, hiding the mountains only a few miles away; or about the desperate, creeping ennui that develops when all the seasons are the same, and it's sunny and warm and pretty and you still feel lonely and depressed, but I think I've made my point. Los Angeles has just as many problems as New York, if not more, once you factor in the cost of moving and trying to create a new life there. It's not the miracle cure for your problems that it presents itself to be. Remember, when it's dead winter and you feel miserable in New York, spring is always on the way, bringing with it new possibilities. Los Angeles can't say that; it can only offer the endless monotony of its seventy-two-degree days, which, to anyone who's lived in New York, will soon feel sad, suffocating, and lifeless.

Don't ever move there!

Best,
Jake

N.B.: Los Angeles forms the template for a number of other sprawling cities out west, from Houston to Phoenix to San Diego, but, as Boston is a pale copy of New York, so are they to LA. Everything I've said here goes double for them.

Dear Jake,

I'm sixty-seven years old and I've lived in New York for all of those years. I've had a great life here—running wild up in the Bronx as a kid, when it was still safe enough to do that; catching the end of the 1960s at City College, when everything was political and all the protests really seemed to matter; getting a teaching job just in time to avoid the Vietnam draft; and, mostly, happily teaching math to high school kids, even during the years when I could have retired with a full pension, something that doesn't exist any more. I was also able to buy a house back when you could do that with only a few years' pay. Now, my kids are grown and settled, and though my wife and I still have plenty of good friends here, each year more and more of them move to warmer climates.

We're thinking about moving down to Florida, too. It's cheaper and warmer, of course, but the main reason is, it feels like the city I once knew and loved has vanished, predeceasing me. All the old mom-and-pop stores, the Jewish delis, and even the big department stores are all gone, along with what seems like whole neighborhoods pulled down and replaced by forty-story-tall condo buildings. Even the parts that remain, like the subway, feel totally different with everyone staring at their phones.

Am I justified in leaving New York when it's already left me?

Sincerely,
An Older Man

Dear AOM:

You should stay in New York until death do you part. This is your home and, despite its many changes, you belong here. Scratch the surface of today's New York, and you'll see the heart and soul of the city remains in all its diversity, excitement, and challenges. Do not generalize from the loss of a few friends to the Sunbelt: The vast majority of New York's million-plus seniors stay put, most in financial and social circumstances far more difficult than your own. They stay for many reasons: family, friends, a routine they don't want to break, but most of all because, contrary to popular opinion, New York actually gets better as you grow older. Best of all, stay and you'll win the prize that the city only awards on death: the badge of being a true, real, native, lifelong New Yorker, which will be mentioned frequently at your funeral.

First, what you say about the city changing is true: Gentrification has worked its terrible magic across nearly every neighborhood. Even in places where the buildings still stand, like the Grand Concourse in the Bronx or the Brownstone Belt in Brooklyn, the population that inhabits them has turned over more than once. But the city has always been like this. From Dutch New Amsterdam to today, each generation has transformed the city, leaving it vastly different by their grandchildren's time.

For centuries, the direction of this change was mainly outward, as the city expanded from the tip of Manhattan to the edges of the five boroughs, and new neighborhoods replaced farmland. By the time of your birth, however, this expansion had reached its natural extent, at least within the city limits, and began reflecting back on itself, churning, burning, and rebuilding old neighborhoods into new ones. Think of all the Italians and Jews sweeping out of the Lower East Side to the Bronx in the early decades of the twentieth century—probably your parents' generation. Think of your kids' generation sweeping right back into the LES: From a certain altitude, it's a beautiful ballet.

There is a natural human tendency to cling to the familiar. To some extent, this is a good thing: Without it, there'd be no countervailing force to gentrification—no neighborhood groups banding together to stop the most outrageous depredations of the market, like replacing the only supermarket with a high-rise luxury tower. But, allowed to grow unchecked, this tendency can lead to rigidity and an opposition to all change, some of which is neutral or even good, like improving safety or building more affordable housing. Look deep and ask yourself, are you really upset that the city has changed, or are you upset that you have not?

Some of our older neighbors do have good reasons to fear change. The elderly are poor compared to the city as a whole, and the majority, who rent their apartments, see their growing rents eat into their fixed incomes year after year. While rent stabilization and various city programs attempt to blunt the impact, for some of our grandparents, the choice is between staying put in increasing poverty or leaving for a southern state where their social-security checks will go further. Luckily, with your pension and home equity, you are not in this group and likely have the disposable income to enjoy some of the upsides of a changed city—the overpriced but better-quality coffee, or the variety of restaurants that didn't exist when you were a kid. No, your problem isn't a real threat so much as just a general discomfort with change, and luckily, that is easy to fix.

Simply put, instead of lamenting what no longer exists, explore the new. I see plenty of my parents' friends out at the new restaurants down on Fifth Avenue in Park Slope, and even a few in the bars, particularly one that has good jazz on Sunday nights. Some truly adventurous sixty- and seventy-somethings even hit the clubs. If that's a little too extreme, what about the cultural scene, which continues to offer an embarrassment of artistic riches, despite the pressure that gentrification has put on struggling artists.

Most of our museums offer free or discount rates for seniors, as well as a multitude of exhibitions from all over the world that could have never been funded in the bad old days. Sure, Broadway shows and movies have grown so expensive that even the well-off can't go as much as they used to, but when you do go, you have so many more options. Even when I was a kid, the nearest movie theater was miles away and had only two screens. Now, thirty years later, there are five swanky multiplexes within walking distance. Some of them don't even have bedbugs! And, if you don't want to walk, you can take the subway where a reduced fare for those over sixty-five is 50 percent off.

If you're lucky enough to own an entire house, you've probably massively benefited from the booming real estate prices over the last twenty years, which means you have the option of trading down to a smaller apartment and using the extra cash to pad out the already good life many NYC seniors enjoy. You could buy a place in Florida and spend the worst part of the winter there, or, better yet, give the money to your kids who probably need it a lot more than you do. Helping them stay in New York, whether by paying for college so they can get a job or helping them out with a down payment for an apartment, is one of the most charitable things you can do, and having your family close by as you age will make New York much more comfortable.

All this can be yours if you just let go of the past. You don't have much time to be depressed when you're busy enjoying a city that gets better every year, and all the time you've been wasting feeling sad for one particular moment in New York's history can be used to actually enjoy the present moment, which, by the way, is the only one that exists. The city is like a phoenix, always burning down and rising from its ashes—harness that energy and you'll be energized right up until to the moment you get hit by that M2 bus at age ninety-five, hopefully while on your bicycle on the way to a sober morning juice rave or something. Your life will be a testament to the tremendous resilience and vitality of New Yorkers, and it will be an example to those of us who will follow you, aiming to stay here, basking in this city's glory, until the very last day of our lives.

See you on the other side,
Jake

N.B.: Those of us who are fortunate enough to live in New York, and not in poverty, have a moral obligation to help out our less fortunate neighbors, particularly the elderly. Whether that's by volunteering or donating to Meals on Wheels, or voting for politicians who make affordable housing for the elderly a priority, we can make this city a better place for our seniors.

Top Ten Best New York Cemeteries

1 **GREEN-WOOD CEMETERY.** The crown jewel of New York graveyards, and almost as big as Prospect Park nearby. You can stroll endlessly looking at all the monuments or climb up Battle Hill to take in one of the best views of the New York Harbor and Statue of Liberty.

2 **NEW YORK MARBLE CEMETERY & NEW YORK CITY MARBLE CEMETERY.** These two small graveyards, off Second Street in the East Village, are strange oases of quiet in an otherwise busy neighborhood; they keep very limited hours, but can also be visited during the annual Open House New York weekend.

3 **WOODLAWN CEMETERY IN THE BRONX.** Similar in size to Green-Wood, this place has dozens of beautiful mausoleums, the graves of many famous artists, musicians, and writers, and one of New York's *Titanic* memorials.

4 **TRINITY CHURCH.** In the shadow of the World Trade Center, this small graveyard survived 9/11 and holds the graves of Alexander Hamilton and many other notables from the early days of the republic.

5 **UPTOWN TRINITY CHURCH CEMETERY.** Made famous by its appearance in *The Royal Tenenbaums*, this hillside graveyard on 155th Street features stunning views of the Hudson River.

6 **CALVARY CEMETERY IN QUEENS.** This is the vast cemetery you see as you drive on the Brooklyn-Queens Expressway, and it's worth a visit for its amazing skyline view of the city.

7 **MACHPELAH CEMETERY IN QUEENS.** Home of Houdini's grave, this tumbling-down graveyard feels near-abandoned except for the strange gifts left for Houdini's spirit: playing cards, candles, locks, and chains.

8 **FRIENDS QUAKER CEMETERY IN PROSPECT PARK.** This burial ground was built almost twenty years before the park grew up around it, and it can still be glimpsed through a fence in the woods behind the ballfields. Rarely open, it still adds an eerie atmosphere to this part of the park.

9 **AFRICAN BURIAL GROUND NATIONAL MONUMENT.** This sacred space on Duane Street, just off Foley Square by the courts downtown, honors the spirits of the fifteen thousand slaves and free black people who were buried there in the seventeenth and eighteenth centuries.

10 **CEMETERIES OF CONGREGATION SHEARITH ISRAEL IN LOWER MANHATTAN.** These three pocket graveyards in Chinatown, the West Village, and Chelsea belong to the oldest Jewish congregation in America; they somehow survived two hundred years of NYC development and remain strangely disjointed from the streets that grew up around them.

Afterword

I've spent this book giving advice about how to live your life in New York City—I hope it will help you lead a happier, more adventurous, and more fulfilling life here. It will not all be smooth sailing, as I've said, but without challenge, there is no growth, and you didn't move here to live a boring life.

This past year, while I was writing these essays, I hit one of those rough periods: I sold Gothamist, saw its new owner shut it down months later after our employees unionized, was vilified in the press for my role in the fiasco, and then, somehow, picked up the pieces and convinced several public radio stations to acquire and relaunch our city websites and rehire many of our staff. And, while my professional life was cycling through these ups and downs, my mom found she had stage-four lung cancer. It was that kind of year.

I tell you this not for sympathy—I've lived a relatively fortunate life compared to most—but because a year like this teaches a person (even a know-it-all native New Yorker) some things, and I wanted to share them with you. First, that despite its gruff and sometimes-unwelcoming exterior, New York can be a surprisingly kind place. Multiple times during this period, I found myself getting stopped on the street by strangers (usually homeless guys) and asked if I was all right, or told "cheer up, it's not the end of the world." When you are in extremis—looking miserable, crying—this side of New York opens to you, and you feel the city's fundamental goodness.

But the rest of the time, when you're just baseline miserable but not looking like you're going to jump in front of a train, the city ignores you. This is a blessed thing. As E. B. White, in his classic essay "Here Is New York," wrote, "On any person who desires such queer prizes, New York will bestow the gift of loneliness and the gift of privacy." That is, despite the crowds of people pressing in everywhere, this city will leave you alone to suffer in peace.

The best life advice I ever received on this topic came from my dad, another native New Yorker who grew up in the Bronx. This was during a different period of tumult in my life. I was twenty-three, was going through a bad breakup, and had dropped out of medical school. At the time, I felt like I had failed in every way and had let everyone in my life down. "Son," he said, "nobody is thinking about you at all—they're all too wrapped up in their own problems to spend any time worrying about yours."

I've thought about this a lot recently. I can't tell you how many days this year I was comforted on the long schlep home from our former office in Midtown to Brooklyn on the B train, just looking around at everyone in the subway car doing their own thing and realizing that all of these people have their troubles. And, despite feeling like my problems were unusual, acute, and terrible, not a single one of them cared. That's the kind of sobering reminder a person needs sometimes: You aren't the center of the world, nor are you alone in your struggle. Breathe. We're all in this together. Try to be useful—and lighten up.

New York was there for me in other ways, of course: I had my incredible wife and forthright friends giving me encouragement that things would get better. I had the restorative urban treasure that is Prospect Park, which I would endlessly circle on my bike, trying to pedal out the stress. During the months when Gothamist was offline, I had time to appreciate parts of New York that I don't usually have time to explore. I spent hours walking around museums, sitting in movie theater matinees, or just wandering miles and miles across the city alone with my thoughts. In good times, New York is really good, but in bad times, New York is even better; it offers myriad ways to pass the time and heal. It's been a few months now, and I love the city more than I ever have before. We've been through something together.

Sooner or later, if you live here long enough, you're going to have one of these years—when your job or personal life or health lurches into a seemingly uncontrollable, fiery tailspin, and I hope you'll be as comforted by New York City as I have been. Likewise, I hope that this book, in a small way, makes you love New York a little bit more, or at least makes it a less confounding place to live. It's a hard city, sometimes, but it's worth it. Don't ever leave.

A native New Yorker,
Jake

Acknowledgments

Many New Yorkers helped me create this book—most especially the readers who sent in so many great questions. Jen Chung, my cofounder at Gothamist, has been my daily sounding board for fifteen years, and she has shared her insightful opinions on every conceivable New York topic with me. John Del Signore, Gothamist's editor in chief, came up with the idea for the column and suggested its name. He also helped edit this book. Jen Carlson, Gothamist's talented and tireless editorial director—who has been with Gothamist almost since the beginning—continues to be an invaluable source of feedback and ideas. Dan Kirschen, my agent, was the first person to suggest that the column could make a book, helped shape the proposal for it, and put up with me during this very insane period of writing it. David Cashion and his team at Abrams were wonderful. Eternal thanks also to my wife and kids who gave me the time to write on weekends and after bedtime, and to my parents who kicked in with babysitting services.

And, finally, much love to the people of the city of New York, who taught me everything I know.